LAWYER'S REFERENCE GUIDES

FAIR CREDIT REPORTING ACT

AS AMENDED THROUGH P.L. 115-174,
ENACTED MAY 24, 2018

UNITED STATES CONGRESS

This Publication is designed to provide accurate and authoritative information in regard to the subject matter covered. It is sold with the understanding that the Publisher is not engaged in rendering legal, accounting, or other professional service. If legal advice or other expert assistance is required, the services of a competent professional should be sought.

Nothing contained herein is intended or written to be used for the purposes of (1) avoiding penalties imposed under the federal Internal Revenue Code, or (2) promoting, marketing, or recommending to another party any transaction or matter addressed herein.

This Publication is provided "as is" and any use by the user is at his or her own risk.

No copyright claim is made to original government works.

A Note to Users

This publication does not represent an official version of any Federal law and should not be cited as legal evidence of the law. It is designed to serve as a reference aid, reproducing updated versions of certain key statutes as maintained by the Office of the Legislative Counsel of the United States Congress.

The official version of Federal law is found in the United States Statutes at Large and in the United States Code (available at http://uscode.house.gov). Before relying solely on the contents of this publication, such official versions should be consulted and appropriate professional advice should be sought.

This publication has a cut off date of June 10, 2019.

This publication is neither authorized nor endorsed by the United States Congress or any governmental body.

FAIR CREDIT REPORTING ACT

[Public Law 90-321; 82 Stat. 146; 15 U.S.C. 1601 et seq.]

[As Amended Through P.L. 115–174, Enacted May 24, 2018]

[Currency: This publication is a compilation of the text of Public Law 90-321. It was last amended by the public law listed in the As Amended Through note above and reflects current law through the date of the enactment of the public law listed at https://www.govinfo.gov/app/collection/comps/]

[Note: While this publication does not represent an official version of any Federal statute, substantial efforts have been made to ensure the accuracy of its contents. The official version of Federal law is found in the United States Statutes at Large and in the United States Code. The legal effect to be given to the Statutes at Large and the United States Code is established by statute (1 U.S.C. 112, 204).]

TITLE VI—CONSUMER CREDIT REPORTING

Sec.
601. Short title.
602. Findings and purpose.
603. Definitions and rules of construction.
604. Permissible purposes of reports.
605. Requirements relating to information contained in consumer reports.
605A. Identity theft prevention; fraud alerts and active duty alerts.
605B. Block of information resulting from identity theft.
606. Disclosure of investigative consumer reports.
607. Compliance procedures.
608. Disclosures to governmental agencies.
609. Disclosure to consumers.
610. Conditions and form of disclosure to consumers.
611. Procedure in case of disputed accuracy.
612. Charges for certain disclosures.
613. Public record information for employment purposes.
614. Restrictions on investigative consumer reports.
615. Requirements on users of consumer reports.
616. Civil liability for willful noncompliance.
617. Civil liability for negligent noncompliance.
618. Jurisdiction of courts; limitation of actions.
619. Obtaining information under false pretenses.
620. Unauthorized disclosures by officers or employees.
621. Administrative enforcement.
622. Information on overdue child support obligations.
623. Responsibilities of furnishers of information to consumer reporting agencies.
624. Affiliate sharing.
625. Relation to State laws.
626. Disclosures to FBI for counterintelligence purposes.
627. Disclosures to governmental agencies for counterintelligence purposes.
628. Disposal of records.
629. Corporate and technological circumvention prohibited.

§ 601. [15 U.S.C. 1601 note] Short title

This title may be cited as the "Fair Credit Reporting Act".

§ 602. [15 U.S.C. 1681] Findings and purpose

(a) The Congress makes the following findings:

(1) The banking system is dependent upon fair and accurate credit reporting. Inaccurate credit reports directly impair the efficiency of the banking system, and unfair credit reporting methods undermine the public confidence which is essential to the continued functioning of the banking system.

(2) An elaborate mechanism has been developed for investigating and evaluating the credit worthiness, credit standing, credit capacity, character, and general reputation of consumers.

(3) Consumer reporting agencies have assumed a vital role in assembling and evaluating consumer credit and other information on consumers.

(4) There is a need to insure that consumer reporting agencies exercise their grave responsibilities with fairness, impartiality, and a respect for the consumer's right to privacy.

(b) It is the purpose of this title to require that consumer reporting agencies adopt reasonable procedures for meeting the needs of commerce for consumer credit, personnel, insurance, and other information in a manner which is fair and equitable to the consumer, with regard to the confidentiality, accuracy, relevancy, and proper utilization of such information in accordance with the requirements of this title.

§ 603. [15 U.S.C. 1681a] Definitions and rules of construction

(a) Definitions and rules of construction set forth in this section are applicable for the purposes of this title.

(b) The term "person" means any individual, partnership, corporation, trust, estate, cooperative, association, government or governmental subdivision or agency, or other entity.

(c) The term "consumer" means an individual.

(d) CONSUMER REPORT.—

(1) IN GENERAL.—The term "consumer report" means any written, oral, or other communication of any information by a consumer reporting agency bearing on a consumer's credit worthiness, credit standing, credit capacity, character, general reputation, personal characteristics, or mode of living which is used or expected to be used or collected in whole or in part for the purpose of serving as a factor in establishing the consumer's eligibility for—

(A) credit or insurance to be used primarily for personal, family, or household purposes;

(B) employment purposes; or

(C) any other purpose authorized under section 604.

(2) EXCLUSIONS.—Except as provided in paragraph (3), the term "consumer report" does not include—

(A) subject to section 624, any—

(i) report containing information solely as to transactions or experiences between the consumer and the person making the report;

(ii) communication of that information among persons related by common ownership or affiliated by corporate control; or

(iii) communication of other information among persons related by common ownership or affiliated by corporate control, if it is clearly and conspicuously disclosed to the consumer that the information may be communicated among such persons and the consumer is given the opportunity, before the time that the information is initially communicated, to direct that such information not be communicated among such persons;

(B) any authorization or approval of a specific extension of credit directly or indirectly by the issuer of a credit card or similar device;

(C) any report in which a person who has been requested by a third party to make a specific extension of credit directly or indirectly to a consumer conveys his or her decision with respect to such request, if the third party advises the consumer of the name and address of the person to whom the request was made, and such person makes the disclosures to the consumer required under section 615; or

(D) a communication described in subsection (o) or (x).

(3) RESTRICTION ON SHARING OF MEDICAL INFORMATION.—Except for information or any communication of information disclosed as provided in section 604(g)(3), the exclusions in paragraph (2) shall not apply with respect to information disclosed to any person related by common ownership or affiliated by corporate control, if the information is—

(A) medical information;

(B) an individualized list or description based on the payment transactions of the consumer for medical products or services; or

(C) an aggregate list of identified consumers based on payment transactions for medical products or services.

(e) The term "investigative consumer report" means a consumer report or portion thereof in which information on a consumer's character, general reputation, personal characteristics, or mode of living is obtained through personal interviews with neighbors, friends, or associates of the consumer reported on or with others with whom he is acquainted or who may have knowledge concerning any such items of information. However, such information shall not include specific factual information on a consumer's credit record obtained directly from a creditor of the consumer or from a consumer reporting agency when such information was obtained directly from a creditor of the consumer or from the consumer.

(f) The term "consumer reporting agency" means any person which, for monetary fees, dues, or on a cooperative nonprofit basis, regularly engages in whole or in part in the practice of assembling or evaluating consumer credit information or other information on consumers for the purpose of furnishing consumer reports to third parties, and which uses any means or facility of interstate commerce for the purpose of preparing or furnishing consumer reports.

(g) The term "file", when used in connection with information on any consumer, means all of the information on that consumer recorded and retained by a consumer reporting agency regardless of how the information is stored.

(h) The term "employment purposes" when used in connection with a consumer report means a report used for the purpose of evaluating a consumer for employment, promotion, reassignment or retention as an employee.

(i) MEDICAL INFORMATION.—The term "medical information"—

(1) means information or data, whether oral or recorded, in any form or medium, created by or derived from a health care provider or the consumer, that relates to—

(A) the past, present, or future physical, mental, or behavioral health or condition of an individual;

(B) the provision of health care to an individual; or

(C) the payment for the provision of health care to an individual.

(2) does not include the age or gender of a consumer, demographic information about the consumer, including a consumer's residence address or e-mail address, or any other information about a consumer that does not relate to the physical, mental, or behavioral health or condition of a consumer, including the existence or value of any insurance policy.

(j) DEFINITIONS RELATING TO CHILD SUPPORT OBLIGATIONS.—

(1) OVERDUE SUPPORT.—The term "overdue support" has the meaning given to such term in section 466(e) of the Social Security Act.

(2) STATE OR LOCAL CHILD SUPPORT ENFORCEMENT AGENCY.—The term "State or local child support enforcement agency" means a State or local agency which administers a State or local program for establishing and enforcing child support obligations.

(k) ADVERSE ACTION.—

(1) ACTIONS INCLUDED.—The term "adverse action"—

(A) has the same meaning as in section 701(d)(6) of the Equal Credit Opportunity Act; and

(B) means—

(i) a denial or cancellation of, an increase in any charge for, or a reduction or other adverse or unfavorable change in the terms of coverage or amount of, any insurance, existing or applied for, in connection with the underwriting of insurance;

(ii) a denial of employment or any other decision for employment purposes that adversely affects any current or prospective employee;

(iii) a denial or cancellation of, an increase in any charge for, or any other adverse or unfavorable change in the terms of, any license or benefit described in section 604(a)(3)(D); and

(iv) an action taken or determination that is—

(I) made in connection with an application that was made by, or a transaction that was initiated by, any consumer, or in connection with a review of an account under section 604(a)(3)(F)(ii); and

(II) adverse to the interests of the consumer.

(2) APPLICABLE FINDINGS, DECISIONS, COMMENTARY, AND ORDERS.—For purposes of any determination of whether an action is an adverse action under paragraph (1)(A), all appropriate final findings, decisions, commentary, and orders issued under section 701(d)(6) of the Equal Credit Opportunity Act by the Bureau or any court shall apply.

(*l*) FIRM OFFER OF CREDIT OR INSURANCE.—The term "firm offer of credit or insurance" means any offer of credit or insurance to a consumer that will be honored if the consumer is determined, based on information in a consumer report on the consumer, to meet the specific criteria used to select the consumer for the offer, except that the offer may be further conditioned on one or more of the following:

(1) The consumer being determined, based on information in the consumer's application for the credit or insurance, to meet specific criteria bearing on credit worthiness or insurability, as applicable, that are established—

(A) before selection of the consumer for the offer; and

(B) for the purpose of determining whether to extend credit or insurance pursuant to the offer.

(2) Verification—

(A) that the consumer continues to meet the specific criteria used to select the consumer for the offer, by using information in a consumer report on the consumer, information in the consumer's application for the credit or insurance, or other information bearing on the credit worthiness or insurability of the consumer; or

(B) of the information in the consumer's application for the credit or insurance, to determine that the consumer meets the specific criteria bearing on credit worthiness or insurability.

(3) The consumer furnishing any collateral that is a requirement for the extension of the credit or insurance that was—

(A) established before selection of the consumer for the offer of credit or insurance; and

(B) disclosed to the consumer in the offer of credit or insurance.

(m) CREDIT OR INSURANCE TRANSACTION THAT IS NOT INITIATED BY THE CONSUMER.—The term "credit or insurance transaction that is not initiated by the consumer" does not include the use of a consumer report by a person with which the consumer has an account or insurance policy, for purposes of—

(1) reviewing the account or insurance policy; or

(2) collecting the account.

(n) STATE.—The term "State" means any State, the Commonwealth of Puerto Rico, the District of Columbia, and any territory or possession of the United States.

(o) EXCLUDED COMMUNICATIONS.—A communication is described in this subsection if it is a communication—

(1) that, but for subsection (d)(2)(D), would be an investigative consumer report;

(2) that is made to a prospective employer for the purpose of—

(A) procuring an employee for the employer; or

(B) procuring an opportunity for a natural person to work for the employer;

(3) that is made by a person who regularly performs such procurement;

(4) that is not used by any person for any purpose other than a purpose described in subparagraph (A) or (B) of paragraph (2); and

(5) with respect to which—

(A) the consumer who is the subject of the communication—

(i) consents orally or in writing to the nature and scope of the communication, before the collection of any information for the purpose of making the communication;

(ii) consents orally or in writing to the making of the communication to a prospective employer, before the making of the communication; and

(iii) in the case of consent under clause (i) or (ii) given orally, is provided written confirmation of that consent by the person making the communication, not later than 3 business days after the receipt of the consent by that person;

(B) the person who makes the communication does not, for the purpose of making the communication, make any inquiry that if made by a prospective employer of the consumer who is the subject of the communication would violate any applicable Federal or State equal employment opportunity law or regulation; and

(C) the person who makes the communication—

(i) discloses in writing to the consumer who is the subject of the communication, not later than 5 business days after receiving any request from the consumer for such disclosure, the nature and substance of all information in the consumer's file at the time of the request, except that the sources of any information that is acquired solely for use in making the communication and is actually used for no other purpose, need not be disclosed other than under appropriate discovery procedures in any court of competent jurisdiction in which an action is brought; and

(ii) notifies the consumer who is the subject of the communication, in writing, of the consumer's right to request the information described in clause (i).

(p) CONSUMER REPORTING AGENCY THAT COMPILES AND MAINTAINS FILES ON CONSUMERS ON A NATIONWIDE BASIS.—The term "consumer reporting agency that compiles and maintains files on consumers on a nationwide basis" means a consumer reporting agency that regularly engages in the practice of assembling or evaluating, and maintaining, for the purpose of furnishing consumer reports to third parties bearing on a consumer's credit worthiness, credit standing, or credit capacity, each of the following regarding consumers residing nationwide:

(1) Public record information.

(2) Credit account information from persons who furnish that information regularly and in the ordinary course of business.

(q) DEFINITIONS RELATING TO FRAUD ALERTS.—

(1) ACTIVE DUTY MILITARY CONSUMER.—The term "active duty military consumer" means a consumer in military service who—

(A) is on active duty (as defined in section 101(d)(1) of title 10, United States Code) or is a reservist performing duty under a call or order to active duty under a provision of law referred to in section 101(a)(13) of title 10, United States Code; and

(B) is assigned to service away from the usual duty station of the consumer.

(2) FRAUD ALERT; ACTIVE DUTY ALERT.—The terms "fraud alert" and "active duty alert" mean a statement in the file of a consumer that—

(A) notifies all prospective users of a consumer report relating to the consumer that the consumer may be a victim of fraud, including identity theft, or is an active duty military consumer, as applicable; and

(B) is presented in a manner that facilitates a clear and conspicuous view of the statement described in subparagraph (A) by any person requesting such consumer report.

(3) IDENTITY THEFT.—The term "identity theft" means a fraud committed using the identifying information of another person, subject to such further definition as the Bureau may prescribe, by regulation.

(4) IDENTITY THEFT REPORT.—The term "identity theft report" has the meaning given that term by rule of the Bureau, and means, at a minimum, a report—

(A) that alleges an identity theft;

(B) that is a copy of an official, valid report filed by a consumer with an appropriate Federal, State, or local law enforcement agency, including the United States Postal Inspection Service, or such other government agency deemed appropriate by the Bureau; and

(C) the filing of which subjects the person filing the report to criminal penalties relating to the filing of false information if, in fact, the information in the report is false.

(5) NEW CREDIT PLAN.—The term "new credit plan" means a new account under an open end credit plan (as defined in section 103(i) of the Truth in Lending Act) or a new credit transaction not under an open end credit plan.

(r) CREDIT AND DEBIT RELATED TERMS—

(1) CARD ISSUER.—The term "card issuer" means—

(A) a credit card issuer, in the case of a credit card; and

(B) a debit card issuer, in the case of a debit card.

(2) CREDIT CARD.—The term "credit card" has the same meaning as in section 103 of the Truth in Lending Act.

(3) DEBIT CARD.—The term "debit card" means any card issued by a financial institution to a consumer for use in initi-

ating an electronic fund transfer from the account of the consumer at such financial institution, for the purpose of transferring money between accounts or obtaining money, property, labor, or services.

(4) ACCOUNT AND ELECTRONIC FUND TRANSFER.—The terms "account" and "electronic fund transfer" have the same meanings as in section 903 of the Electronic Fund Transfer Act.

(5) CREDIT AND CREDITOR.—The terms "credit" and "creditor" have the same meanings as in section 702 of the Equal Credit Opportunity Act.

(s) FEDERAL BANKING AGENCY.—The term "Federal banking agency" has the same meaning as in section 3 of the Federal Deposit Insurance Act.

(t) FINANCIAL INSTITUTION.—The term "financial institution" means a State or National bank, a State or Federal savings and loan association, a mutual savings bank, a State or Federal credit union, or any other person that, directly or indirectly, holds a transaction account (as defined in section 19(b) of the Federal Reserve Act) belonging to a consumer.

(u) RESELLER.—The term "reseller" means a consumer reporting agency that—

(1) assembles and merges information contained in the database of another consumer reporting agency or multiple consumer reporting agencies concerning any consumer for purposes of furnishing such information to any third party, to the extent of such activities; and

(2) does not maintain a database of the assembled or merged information from which new consumer reports are produced.

(v) COMMISSION.—The term "Commission" means the Bureau.

(w) The term "Bureau" means the Bureau of Consumer Financial Protection.

(x) NATIONWIDE SPECIALTY CONSUMER REPORTING AGENCY.—The term "nationwide specialty consumer reporting agency" means a consumer reporting agency that compiles and maintains files on consumers on a nationwide basis relating to—

(1) medical records or payments;
(2) residential or tenant history;
(3) check writing history;
(4) employment history; or
(5) insurance claims.

(y) EXCLUSION OF CERTAIN COMMUNICATIONS FOR EMPLOYEE INVESTIGATIONS.—

(1) COMMUNICATIONS DESCRIBED IN THIS SUBSECTION.—A communication is described in this subsection if—

(A) but for subsection (d)(2)(D), the communication would be a consumer report;

(B) the communication is made to an employer in connection with an investigation of—

(i) suspected misconduct relating to employment; or

(ii) compliance with Federal, State, or local laws and regulations, the rules of a self-regulatory organization, or any preexisting written policies of the employer;

(C) the communication is not made for the purpose of investigating a consumer's credit worthiness, credit standing, or credit capacity; and

(D) the communication is not provided to any person except—

(i) to the employer or an agent of the employer;

(ii) to any Federal or State officer, agency, or department, or any officer, agency, or department of a unit of general local government;

(iii) to any self-regulatory organization with regulatory authority over the activities of the employer or employee;

(iv) as otherwise required by law; or

(v) pursuant to section 608.

(2) SUBSEQUENT DISCLOSURE.—After taking any adverse action based in whole or in part on a communication described in paragraph (1), the employer shall disclose to the consumer a summary containing the nature and substance of the communication upon which the adverse action is based, except that the sources of information acquired solely for use in preparing what would be but for subsection (d)(2)(D) an investigative consumer report need not be disclosed.

(3) SELF-REGULATORY ORGANIZATION DEFINED.—For purposes of this subsection, the term "self-regulatory organization" includes any self-regulatory organization (as defined in section 3(a)(26) of the Securities Exchange Act of 1934), any entity established under title I of the Sarbanes-Oxley Act of 2002, any board of trade designated by the Commodity Futures Trading Commission, and any futures association registered with such Commission.

(z) VETERAN.—The term "veteran" has the meaning given the term in section 101 of title 38, United States Code.

(aa) VETERAN'S MEDICAL DEBT.—The term "veteran's medical debt"—

(1) means a medical collection debt of a veteran owed to a non-Department of Veterans Affairs health care provider that was submitted to the Department for payment for health care authorized by the Department of Veterans Affairs; and

(2) includes medical collection debt that the Department of Veterans Affairs has wrongfully charged a veteran.

§ 604. [15 U.S.C. 1681b] Permissible purposes of reports

(a) IN GENERAL.—Subject to subsection (c), any consumer reporting agency may furnish a consumer report under the following circumstances and no other:

(1) In response to the order of a court having jurisdiction to issue such an order, or a subpoena issued in connection with proceedings before a Federal grand jury.

(2) In accordance with the written instructions of the consumer to whom it relates.

(3) To a person which it has reason to believe—

(A) intends to use the information in connection with a credit transaction involving the consumer on whom the information is to be furnished and involving the extension of credit to, or review or collection of an account of, the consumer; or

(B) intends to use the information for employment purposes; or

(C) intends to use the information in connection with the underwriting of insurance involving the consumer; or

(D) intends to use the information in connection with a determination of the consumer's eligibility for a license or other benefit granted by a governmental instrumentality required by law to consider an applicant's financial responsibility or status; or

(E) intends to use the information, as a potential investor or servicer, or current insurer, in connection with a valuation of, or an assessment of the credit or prepayment risks associated with, an existing credit obligation; or

(F) otherwise has a legitimate business need for the information—

(i) in connection with a business transaction that is initiated by the consumer; or

(ii) to review an account to determine whether the consumer continues to meet the terms of the account.

(G) executive departments and agencies in connection with the issuance of government-sponsored individually-billed travel charge cards.

(4) In response to a request by the head of a State or local child support enforcement agency (or a State or local government official authorized by the head of such an agency), if the person making the request certifies to the consumer reporting agency that—

(A) the consumer report is needed for the purpose of establishing an individual's capacity to make child support payments, determining the appropriate level of such payments, or enforcing a child support order, award, agreement, or judgment;

(B) the parentage of the consumer for the child to which the obligation relates has been established or acknowledged by the consumer in accordance with State laws under which the obligation arises (if required by those laws); and

(C) the consumer report will be kept confidential, will be used solely for a purpose described in subparagraph (A), and will not be used in connection with any other civil, administrative, or criminal proceeding, or for any other purpose.

(5) To an agency administering a State plan under section 454 of the Social Security Act (42 U.S.C. 654) for use to set an initial or modified child support award.

(6) To the Federal Deposit Insurance Corporation or the National Credit Union Administration as part of its preparation for its appointment or as part of its exercise of powers, as conservator, receiver, or liquidating agent for an insured de-

pository institution or insured credit union under the Federal Deposit Insurance Act or the Federal Credit Union Act, or other applicable Federal or State law, or in connection with the resolution or liquidation of a failed or failing insured depository institution or insured credit union, as applicable.

(b) CONDITIONS FOR FURNISHING AND USING CONSUMER REPORTS FOR EMPLOYMENT PURPOSES.—

(1) CERTIFICATION FROM USER.—A consumer reporting agency may furnish a consumer report for employment purposes only if—

(A) the person who obtains such report from the agency certifies to the agency that—

(i) the person has complied with paragraph (2) with respect to the consumer report, and the person will comply with paragraph (3) with respect to the consumer report if paragraph (3) becomes applicable; and

(ii) information from the consumer report will not be used in violation of any applicable Federal or State equal employment opportunity law or regulation; and

(B) the consumer reporting agency provides with the report, or has previously provided, a summary of the consumer's rights under this title, as prescribed by the Bureau under section 609(c)(3).

(2) DISCLOSURE TO CONSUMER.—

(A) IN GENERAL.—Except as provided in subparagraph (B), a person may not procure a consumer report, or cause a consumer report to be procured, for employment purposes with respect to any consumer, unless—

(i) a clear and conspicuous disclosure has been made in writing to the consumer at any time before the report is procured or caused to be procured, in a document that consists solely of the disclosure, that a consumer report may be obtained for employment purposes; and

(ii) the consumer has authorized in writing (which authorization may be made on the document referred to in clause (i)) the procurement of the report by that person.

(B) APPLICATION BY MAIL, TELEPHONE, COMPUTER, OR OTHER SIMILAR MEANS.—If a consumer described in subparagraph (C) applies for employment by mail, telephone, computer, or other similar means, at any time before a consumer report is procured or caused to be procured in connection with that application—

(i) the person who procures the consumer report on the consumer for employment purposes shall provide to the consumer, by oral, written, or electronic means, notice that a consumer report may be obtained for employment purposes, and a summary of the consumer's rights under section 615(a)(3); and

(ii) the consumer shall have consented, orally, in writing, or electronically to the procurement of the report by that person.

(C) SCOPE.—Subparagraph (B) shall apply to a person procuring a consumer report on a consumer in connection with the consumer's application for employment only if—

(i) the consumer is applying for a position over which the Secretary of Transportation has the power to establish qualifications and maximum hours of service pursuant to the provisions of section 31502 of title 49, or a position subject to safety regulation by a State transportation agency; and

(ii) as of the time at which the person procures the report or causes the report to be procured the only interaction between the consumer and the person in connection with that employment application has been by mail, telephone, computer, or other similar means.

(3) CONDITIONS ON USE FOR ADVERSE ACTIONS.—

(A) IN GENERAL.—Except as provided in subparagraph (B), in using a consumer report for employment purposes, before taking any adverse action based in whole or in part on the report, the person intending to take such adverse action shall provide to the consumer to whom the report relates—

(i) a copy of the report; and

(ii) a description in writing of the rights of the consumer under this title, as prescribed by the Bureau under section 609(c)(3).

(B) APPLICATION BY MAIL, TELEPHONE, COMPUTER, OR OTHER SIMILAR MEANS.—

(i) If a consumer described in subparagraph (C) applies for employment by mail, telephone, computer, or other similar means, and if a person who has procured a consumer report on the consumer for employment purposes takes adverse action on the employment application based in whole or in part on the report, then the person must provide to the consumer to whom the report relates, in lieu of the notices required under subparagraph (A) of this section and under section 615(a), within 3 business days of taking such action, an oral, written or electronic notification—

(I) that adverse action has been taken based in whole or in part on a consumer report received from a consumer reporting agency;

(II) of the name, address and telephone number of the consumer reporting agency that furnished the consumer report (including a toll-free telephone number established by the agency if the agency compiles and maintains files on consumers on a nationwide basis);

(III) that the consumer reporting agency did not make the decision to take the adverse action and is unable to provide to the consumer the specific reasons why the adverse action was taken; and

(IV) that the consumer may, upon providing proper identification, request a free copy of a report and may dispute with the consumer reporting agency the accuracy or completeness of any information in a report.

(ii) If, under clause (B)(i)(IV), the consumer requests a copy of a consumer report from the person who procured the report, then, within 3 business days of receiving the consumer's request, together with proper identification, the person must send or provide to the consumer a copy of a report and a copy of the consumer's rights as prescribed by the Bureau under section 609(c)(3).

(C) SCOPE.—Subparagraph (B) shall apply to a person procuring a consumer report on a consumer in connection with the consumer's application for employment only if—

(i) the consumer is applying for a position over which the Secretary of Transportation has the power to establish qualifications and maximum hours of service pursuant to the provisions of section 31502 of title 49, or a position subject to safety regulation by a State transportation agency; and

(ii) as of the time at which the person procures the report or causes the report to be procured the only interaction between the consumer and the person in connection with that employment application has been by mail, telephone, computer, or other similar means.

(4) EXCEPTION FOR NATIONAL SECURITY INVESTIGATIONS.—

(A) IN GENERAL.—In the case of an agency or department of the United States Government which seeks to obtain and use a consumer report for employment purposes, paragraph (3) shall not apply to any adverse action by such agency or department which is based in part on such consumer report, if the head of such agency or department makes a written finding that—

(i) the consumer report is relevant to a national security investigation of such agency or department;

(ii) the investigation is within the jurisdiction of such agency or department;

(iii) there is reason to believe that compliance with paragraph (3) will—

(I) endanger the life or physical safety of any person;

(II) result in flight from prosecution;

(III) result in the destruction of, or tampering with, evidence relevant to the investigation;

(IV) result in the intimidation of a potential witness relevant to the investigation;

(V) result in the compromise of classified information; or

(VI) otherwise seriously jeopardize or unduly delay the investigation or another official proceeding.

(B) NOTIFICATION OF CONSUMER UPON CONCLUSION OF INVESTIGATION.—Upon the conclusion of a national security investigation described in subparagraph (A), or upon the determination that the exception under subparagraph (A) is no longer required for the reasons set forth in such subparagraph, the official exercising the authority in such subparagraph shall provide to the consumer who is the subject of the consumer report with regard to which such finding was made—

    (i) a copy of such consumer report with any classified information redacted as necessary;

    (ii) notice of any adverse action which is based, in part, on the consumer report; and

    (iii) the identification with reasonable specificity of the nature of the investigation for which the consumer report was sought.

(C) DELEGATION BY HEAD OF AGENCY OR DEPARTMENT.—For purposes of subparagraphs (A) and (B), the head of any agency or department of the United States Government may delegate his or her authorities under this paragraph to an official of such agency or department who has personnel security responsibilities and is a member of the Senior Executive Service or equivalent civilian or military rank.

(D) DEFINITIONS.—For purposes of this paragraph, the following definitions shall apply:

    (i) CLASSIFIED INFORMATION.—The term "classified information" means information that is protected from unauthorized disclosure under Executive Order No. 12958 or successor orders.

    (ii) NATIONAL SECURITY INVESTIGATION.—The term "national security investigation" means any official inquiry by an agency or department of the United States Government to determine the eligibility of a consumer to receive access or continued access to classified information or to determine whether classified information has been lost or compromised.

(c) FURNISHING REPORTS IN CONNECTION WITH CREDIT OR INSURANCE TRANSACTIONS THAT ARE NOT INITIATED BY THE CONSUMER.—

(1) IN GENERAL.—A consumer reporting agency may furnish a consumer report relating to any consumer pursuant to subparagraph (A) or (C) of subsection (a)(3) in connection with any credit or insurance transaction that is not initiated by the consumer only if—

    (A) the consumer authorizes the agency to provide such report to such person; or

    (B)(i) the transaction consists of a firm offer of credit or insurance;

    (ii) the consumer reporting agency has complied with subsection (e);

    (iii) there is not in effect an election by the consumer, made in accordance with subsection (e), to have the consumer's name and address excluded from lists of names provided by the agency pursuant to this paragraph; and

    (iv) the consumer report does not contain a date of birth that shows that the consumer has not attained the age of 21, or, if the date of birth on the consumer report shows that the consumer has not attained the age of 21, such consumer consents to the consumer reporting agency to such furnishing.

(2) LIMITS ON INFORMATION RECEIVED UNDER PARAGRAPH (1)(B).—A person may receive pursuant to paragraph (1)(B) only—

(A) the name and address of a consumer;

(B) an identifier that is not unique to the consumer and that is used by the person solely for the purpose of verifying the identity of the consumer; and

(C) other information pertaining to a consumer that does not identify the relationship or experience of the consumer with respect to a particular creditor or other entity.

(3) INFORMATION REGARDING INQUIRIES.—Except as provided in section 609(a)(5), a consumer reporting agency shall not furnish to any person a record of inquiries in connection with a credit or insurance transaction that is not initiated by a consumer.

(d) RESERVED.

(e) ELECTION OF CONSUMER TO BE EXCLUDED FROM LISTS.—

(1) IN GENERAL.—A consumer may elect to have the consumer's name and address excluded from any list provided by a consumer reporting agency under subsection (c)(1)(B) in connection with a credit or insurance transaction that is not initiated by the consumer by notifying the agency in accordance with paragraph (2) that the consumer does not consent to any use of a consumer report relating to the consumer in connection with any credit or insurance transaction that is not initiated by the consumer.

(2) MANNER OF NOTIFICATION.—A consumer shall notify a consumer reporting agency under paragraph (1)—

(A) through the notification system maintained by the agency under paragraph (5); or

(B) by submitting to the agency a signed notice of election form issued by the agency for purposes of this subparagraph.

(3) RESPONSE OF AGENCY AFTER NOTIFICATION THROUGH SYSTEM.—Upon receipt of notification of the election of a consumer under paragraph (1) through the notification system maintained by the agency under paragraph (5), a consumer reporting agency shall—

(A) inform the consumer that the election is effective only for the 5-year period following the election if the consumer does not submit to the agency a signed notice of election form issued by the agency for purposes of paragraph (2)(B); and

(B) provide to the consumer a notice of election form, if requested by the consumer, not later than 5 business days after receipt of the notification of the election through the system established under paragraph (5), in the case of a request made at the time the consumer provides notification through the system.

(4) EFFECTIVENESS OF ELECTION.—An election of a consumer under paragraph (1)—

(A) shall be effective with respect to a consumer reporting agency beginning 5 business days after the date on which the consumer notifies the agency in accordance with paragraph (2);

(B) shall be effective with respect to a consumer reporting agency—

(i) subject to subparagraph (C), during the 5-year period beginning 5 business days after the date on which the consumer notifies the agency of the election, in the case of an election for which a consumer notifies the agency only in accordance with paragraph (2)(A); or

(ii) until the consumer notifies the agency under subparagraph (C), in the case of an election for which a consumer notifies the agency in accordance with paragraph (2)(B);

(C) shall not be effective after the date on which the consumer notifies the agency, through the notification system established by the agency under paragraph (5), that the election is no longer effective; and

(D) shall be effective with respect to each affiliate of the agency.

(5) NOTIFICATION SYSTEM.—

(A) IN GENERAL.—Each consumer reporting agency that, under subsection (c)(1)(B), furnishes a consumer report in connection with a credit or insurance transaction that is not initiated by a consumer shall—

(i) establish and maintain a notification system, including a toll-free telephone number, which permits any consumer whose consumer report is maintained by the agency to notify the agency, with appropriate identification, of the consumer's election to have the consumer's name and address excluded from any such list of names and addresses provided by the agency for such a transaction; and

(ii) publish by not later than 365 days after the date of enactment of the Consumer Credit Reporting Reform Act of 1996, and not less than annually thereafter, in a publication of general circulation in the area served by the agency—

(I) a notification that information in consumer files maintained by the agency may be used in connection with such transactions; and

(II) the address and toll-free telephone number for consumers to use to notify the agency of the consumer's election under clause (i).

(B) ESTABLISHMENT AND MAINTENANCE AS COMPLIANCE.—Establishment and maintenance of a notification system (including a toll-free telephone number) and publication by a consumer reporting agency on the agency's own behalf and on behalf of any of its affiliates in accordance with this paragraph is deemed to be compliance with this paragraph by each of those affiliates.

(6) NOTIFICATION SYSTEM BY AGENCIES THAT OPERATE NATIONWIDE.—Each consumer reporting agency that compiles and maintains files on consumers on a nationwide basis shall establish and maintain a notification system for purposes of paragraph (5) jointly with other such consumer reporting agencies.

(f) CERTAIN USE OR OBTAINING OF INFORMATION PROHIBITED.—A person shall not use or obtain a consumer report for any purpose unless—

(1) the consumer report is obtained for a purpose for which the consumer report is authorized to be furnished under this section; and

(2) the purpose is certified in accordance with section 607 by a prospective user of the report through a general or specific certification.

(g) PROTECTION OF MEDICAL INFORMATION.—

(1) LIMITATION ON CONSUMER REPORTING AGENCIES.—A consumer reporting agency shall not furnish for employment purposes, or in connection with a credit or insurance transaction, a consumer report that contains medical information (other than medical contact information treated in the manner required under section 605(a)(6)) about a consumer, unless—

(A) if furnished in connection with an insurance transaction, the consumer affirmatively consents to the furnishing of the report;

(B) if furnished for employment purposes or in connection with a credit transaction—

(i) the information to be furnished is relevant to process or effect the employment or credit transaction; and

(ii) the consumer provides specific written consent for the furnishing of the report that describes in clear and conspicuous language the use for which the information will be furnished; or

(C) the information to be furnished pertains solely to transactions, accounts, or balances relating to debts arising from the receipt of medical services, products, or devises, where such information, other than account status or amounts, is restricted or reported using codes that do not identify, or do not provide information sufficient to infer, the specific provider or the nature of such services, products, or devices, as provided in section 605(a)(6).

(2) LIMITATION ON CREDITORS.—Except as permitted pursuant to paragraph (3)(C) or regulations prescribed under paragraph (5)(A), a creditor shall not obtain or use medical information (other than medical information treated in the manner required under section 605(a)(6)) pertaining to a consumer in connection with any determination of the consumer's eligibility, or continued eligibility, for credit.

(3) ACTIONS AUTHORIZED BY FEDERAL LAW, INSURANCE ACTIVITIES AND REGULATORY DETERMINATIONS.—Section 603(d)(3) shall not be construed so as to treat information or any com-

munication of information as a consumer report if the information or communication is disclosed—

(A) in connection with the business of insurance or annuities, including the activities described in section 18B of the model Privacy of Consumer Financial and Health Information Regulation issued by the National Association of Insurance Commissioners (as in effect on January 1, 2003);

(B) for any purpose permitted without authorization under the Standards for Individually Identifiable Health Information promulgated by the Department of Health and Human Services pursuant to the Health Insurance Portability and Accountability Act of 1996, or referred to under section 1179 of such Act, or described in section 502(e) of Public Law 106–102; or

(C) as otherwise determined to be necessary and appropriate, by regulation or order, by the Bureau or the applicable State insurance authority (with respect to any person engaged in providing insurance or annuities).

(4) LIMITATION ON REDISCLOSURE OF MEDICAL INFORMATION.—Any person that receives medical information pursuant to paragraph (1) or (3) shall not disclose such information to any other person, except as necessary to carry out the purpose for which the information was initially disclosed, or as otherwise permitted by statute, regulation, or order.

(5) REGULATIONS AND EFFECTIVE DATE FOR PARAGRAPH (2).—

(A)[1] REGULATIONS REQUIRED.—The Bureau may, after notice and opportunity for comment, prescribe regulations that permit transactions under paragraph (2) that are determined to be necessary and appropriate to protect legitimate operational, transactional, risk, consumer, and other needs (and which shall include permitting actions necessary for administrative verification purposes), consistent with the intent of paragraph (2) to restrict the use of medical information for inappropriate purposes.

(6) COORDINATION WITH OTHER LAWS.—No provision of this subsection shall be construed as altering, affecting, or superseding the applicability of any other provision of Federal law relating to medical confidentiality.

§ 605. [15 U.S.C. 1681c] Requirements relating to information contained in consumer reports

(a) INFORMATION EXCLUDED FROM CONSUMER REPORTS.—Except as authorized under subsection (b), no consumer reporting agency may make any consumer report containing any of the following items of information:

(1) Cases under title 11 of the United States Code or under the Bankruptcy Act that, from the date of entry of the order for relief or the date of adjudication, as the case may be, antedate the report by more than 10 years.

---

[1] So in law. There is no subparagraph (B). See amendment made by section 1088(a)(4)(B) of Public Law 111–203.

(2) Civil suits, civil judgments, and records of arrest that, from date of entry, antedate the report by more than seven years or until the governing statute of limitations has expired, whichever is the longer period.

(3) Paid tax liens which, from date of payment, antedate the report by more than seven years.

(4) Accounts placed for collection or charged to profit and loss which antedate the report by more than seven years.

(5) Any other adverse item of information, other than records of convictions of crimes which antedates the report by more than seven years.

(6) The name, address, and telephone number of any medical information furnisher that has notified the agency of its status, unless—

> (A) such name, address, and telephone number are restricted or reported using codes that do not identify, or provide information sufficient to infer, the specific provider or the nature of such services, products, or devices to a person other than the consumer; or
>
> (B) the report is being provided to an insurance company for a purpose relating to engaging in the business of insurance other than property and casualty insurance.

(7) With respect to a consumer reporting agency described in section 603(p), any information related to a veteran's medical debt if the date on which the hospital care, medical services, or extended care services was rendered relating to the debt antedates the report by less than 1 year if the consumer reporting agency has actual knowledge that the information is related to a veteran's medical debt and the consumer reporting agency is in compliance with its obligation under section 302(c)(5) of the Economic Growth, Regulatory Relief, and Consumer Protection Act.

(8) With respect to a consumer reporting agency described in section 603(p), any information related to a fully paid or settled veteran's medical debt that had been characterized as delinquent, charged off, or in collection if the consumer reporting agency has actual knowledge that the information is related to a veteran's medical debt and the consumer reporting agency is in compliance with its obligation under section 302(c)(5) of the Economic Growth, Regulatory Relief, and Consumer Protection Act.

(b) The provisions of paragraphs (1) through (5) of subsection (a) are not applicable in the case of any consumer credit report to be used in connection with—

> (1) a credit transaction involving, or which may reasonably be expected to involve, a principal amount of $150,000 or more;
>
> (2) the underwriting of life insurance involving, or which may reasonably be expected to involve, a face amount of $150,000 or more; or
>
> (3) the employment of any individual at an annual salary which equals, or which may reasonably be expected to equal $75,000, or more.

(c) RUNNING OF REPORTING PERIOD.—

(1) IN GENERAL.—The 7-year period referred to in paragraphs (4) and (6) of subsection (a) shall begin, with respect to any delinquent account that is placed for collection (internally or by referral to a third party, whichever is earlier), charged to profit and loss, or subjected to any similar action, upon the expiration of the 180-day period beginning on the date of the commencement of the delinquency which immediately preceded the collection activity, charge to profit and loss, or similar action.

(2) EFFECTIVE DATE.—Paragraph (1) shall apply only to items of information added to the file of a consumer on or after the date that is 455 days after the date of enactment of the Consumer Credit Reporting Reform Act of 1996.

(d) INFORMATION REQUIRED TO BE DISCLOSED.—

(1) TITLE 11 INFORMATION.—Any consumer reporting agency that furnishes a consumer report that contains information regarding any case involving the consumer that arises under title 11, United States Code, shall include in the report an identification of the chapter of such title 11 under which such case arises if provided by the source of the information. If any case arising or filed under title 11, United States Code, is withdrawn by the consumer before a final judgment, the consumer reporting agency shall include in the report that such case or filing was withdrawn upon receipt of documentation certifying such withdrawal.

(2) KEY FACTOR IN CREDIT SCORE INFORMATION.—Any consumer reporting agency that furnishes a consumer report that contains any credit score or any other risk score or predictor on any consumer shall include in the report a clear and conspicuous statement that a key factor (as defined in section 609(f)(2)(B)) that adversely affected such score or predictor was the number of enquiries, if such a predictor was in fact a key factor that adversely affected such score. This paragraph shall not apply to a check services company, acting as such, which issues authorizations for the purpose of approving or processing negotiable instruments, electronic fund transfers, or similar methods of payments, but only to the extent that such company is engaged in such activities.

(e) INDICATION OF CLOSURE OF ACCOUNT BY CONSUMER.—If a consumer reporting agency is notified pursuant to section 623(a)(4) that a credit account of a consumer was voluntarily closed by the consumer, the agency shall indicate that fact in any consumer report that includes information related to the account.

(f) INDICATION OF DISPUTE BY CONSUMER.—If a consumer reporting agency is notified pursuant to section 623(a)(3) that information regarding a consumer who was furnished to the agency is disputed by the consumer, the agency shall indicate that fact in each consumer report that includes the disputed information.

(g) TRUNCATION OF CREDIT CARD AND DEBIT CARD NUMBERS.—

(1) IN GENERAL.—Except as otherwise provided in this subsection, no person that accepts credit cards or debit cards for the transaction of business shall print more than the last 5 digits of the card number or the expiration date upon any re-

ceipt provided to the cardholder at the point of the sale or transaction.

(2) LIMITATION.—This subsection shall apply only to receipts that are electronically printed, and shall not apply to transactions in which the sole means of recording a credit card or debit card account number is by handwriting or by an imprint or copy of the card.

(3) EFFECTIVE DATE.—This subsection shall become effective—

(A) 3 years after the date of enactment of this subsection, with respect to any cash register or other machine or device that electronically prints receipts for credit card or debit card transactions that is in use before January 1, 2005; and

(B) 1 year after the date of enactment of this subsection, with respect to any cash register or other machine or device that electronically prints receipts for credit card or debit card transactions that is first put into use on or after January 1, 2005.

(h) NOTICE OF DISCREPANCY IN ADDRESS.—

(1) IN GENERAL.—If a person has requested a consumer report relating to a consumer from a consumer reporting agency described in section 603(p), the request includes an address for the consumer that substantially differs from the addresses in the file of the consumer, and the agency provides a consumer report in response to the request, the consumer reporting agency shall notify the requester of the existence of the discrepancy.

(2) REGULATIONS.—

(A) REGULATIONS REQUIRED.—The Bureau shall,,[2] in consultation with the Federal banking agencies, the National Credit Union Administration, and the Federal Trade Commission,,[78] prescribe regulations providing guidance regarding reasonable policies and procedures that a user of a consumer report should employ when such user has received a notice of discrepancy under paragraph (1).

(B) POLICIES AND PROCEDURES TO BE INCLUDED.—The regulations prescribed under subparagraph (A) shall describe reasonable policies and procedures for use by a user of a consumer report—

(i) to form a reasonable belief that the user knows the identity of the person to whom the consumer report pertains; and

(ii) if the user establishes a continuing relationship with the consumer, and the user regularly and in the ordinary course of business furnishes information to the consumer reporting agency from which the notice of discrepancy pertaining to the consumer was obtained, to reconcile the address of the consumer with the consumer reporting agency by furnishing such address to such consumer reporting agency as part of information regularly furnished by the user for the period in which the relationship is established.

---

[2] So in law.

§ 605A. [15 U.S.C. 1681c–1] Identity theft prevention; fraud alerts and active duty alerts

(a) ONE-CALL FRAUD ALERTS.—

(1) INITIAL ALERTS.—Upon the direct request of a consumer, or an individual acting on behalf of or as a personal representative of a consumer, who asserts in good faith a suspicion that the consumer has been or is about to become a victim of fraud or related crime, including identity theft, a consumer reporting agency described in section 603(p) that maintains a file on the consumer and has received appropriate proof of the identity of the requester shall—

(A) include a fraud alert in the file of that consumer, and also provide that alert along with any credit score generated in using that file, for a period of not less than 1 year, beginning on the date of such request, unless the consumer or such representative requests that such fraud alert be removed before the end of such period, and the agency has received appropriate proof of the identity of the requester for such purpose; and

(B) refer the information regarding the fraud alert under this paragraph to each of the other consumer reporting agencies described in section 603(p), in accordance with procedures developed under section 621(f).

(2) ACCESS TO FREE REPORTS.—In any case in which a consumer reporting agency includes a fraud alert in the file of a consumer pursuant to this subsection, the consumer reporting agency shall—

(A) disclose to the consumer that the consumer may request a free copy of the file of the consumer pursuant to section 612(d); and

(B) provide to the consumer all disclosures required to be made under section 609, without charge to the consumer, not later than 3 business days after any request described in subparagraph (A).

(b) EXTENDED ALERTS.—

(1) IN GENERAL.—Upon the direct request of a consumer, or an individual acting on behalf of or as a personal representative of a consumer, who submits an identity theft report to a consumer reporting agency described in section 603(p) that maintains a file on the consumer, if the agency has received appropriate proof of the identity of the requester, the agency shall—

(A) include a fraud alert in the file of that consumer, and also provide that alert along with any credit score generated in using that file, during the 7-year period beginning on the date of such request, unless the consumer or such representative requests that such fraud alert be removed before the end of such period and the agency has received appropriate proof of the identity of the requester for such purpose;

(B) during the 5-year period beginning on the date of such request, exclude the consumer from any list of consumers prepared by the consumer reporting agency and provided to any third party to offer credit or insurance to the consumer as part of a transaction that was not initiated by the consumer, unless the consumer or such representative requests that such exclusion be rescinded before the end of such period; and

(C) refer the information regarding the extended fraud alert under this paragraph to each of the other consumer reporting agencies described in section 603(p), in accordance with procedures developed under section 621(f).

(2) ACCESS TO FREE REPORTS.—In any case in which a consumer reporting agency includes a fraud alert in the file of a consumer pursuant to this subsection, the consumer reporting agency shall—

(A) disclose to the consumer that the consumer may request 2 free copies of the file of the consumer pursuant to section 612(d) during the 12-month period beginning on the date on which the fraud alert was included in the file; and

(B) provide to the consumer all disclosures required to be made under section 609, without charge to the consumer, not later than 3 business days after any request described in subparagraph (A).

(c) ACTIVE DUTY ALERTS.—Upon the direct request of an active duty military consumer, or an individual acting on behalf of or as a personal representative of an active duty military consumer, a consumer reporting agency described in section 603(p) that maintains a file on the active duty military consumer and has received appropriate proof of the identity of the requester shall—

(1) include an active duty alert in the file of that active duty military consumer, and also provide that alert along with any credit score generated in using that file, during a period of not less than 12 months, or such longer period as the Bureau shall determine, by regulation, beginning on the date of the request, unless the active duty military consumer or such representative requests that such fraud alert be removed before the end of such period, and the agency has received appropriate proof of the identity of the requester for such purpose;

(2) during the 2-year period beginning on the date of such request, exclude the active duty military consumer from any list of consumers prepared by the consumer reporting agency and provided to any third party to offer credit or insurance to the consumer as part of a transaction that was not initiated by the consumer, unless the consumer requests that such exclusion be rescinded before the end of such period; and

(3) refer the information regarding the active duty alert to each of the other consumer reporting agencies described in section 603(p), in accordance with procedures developed under section 621(f).

(d) PROCEDURES.—Each consumer reporting agency described in section 603(p) shall establish policies and procedures to comply with this section, including procedures that inform consumers of the availability of initial, extended, and active duty alerts and procedures that allow consumers and active duty military consumers to request initial, extended, or active duty alerts (as applicable) in a simple and easy manner, including by telephone.

(e) REFERRALS OF ALERTS.—Each consumer reporting agency described in section 603(p) that receives a referral of a fraud alert or active duty alert from another consumer reporting agency pursuant to this section shall, as though the agency received the request from the consumer directly, follow the procedures required under—

(1) paragraphs (1)(A) and (2) of subsection (a), in the case of a referral under subsection (a)(1)(B);

(2) paragraphs (1)(A), (1)(B), and (2) of subsection (b), in the case of a referral under subsection (b)(1)(C); and

(3) paragraphs (1) and (2) of subsection (c), in the case of a referral under subsection (c)(3).

(f) DUTY OF RESELLER TO RECONVEY ALERT.—A reseller shall include in its report any fraud alert or active duty alert placed in the file of a consumer pursuant to this section by another consumer reporting agency.

(g) DUTY OF OTHER CONSUMER REPORTING AGENCIES TO PROVIDE CONTACT INFORMATION.—If a consumer contacts any consumer reporting agency that is not described in section 603(p) to communicate a suspicion that the consumer has been or is about to become a victim of fraud or related crime, including identity theft, the agency shall provide information to the consumer on how to contact the Bureau and the consumer reporting agencies described in section 603(p) to obtain more detailed information and request alerts under this section.

(h) LIMITATIONS ON USE OF INFORMATION FOR CREDIT EXTENSIONS.—

(1) REQUIREMENTS FOR INITIAL AND ACTIVE DUTY ALERTS.—

(A) NOTIFICATION.—Each initial fraud alert and active duty alert under this section shall include information that notifies all prospective users of a consumer report on the consumer to which the alert relates that the consumer does not authorize the establishment of any new credit plan or extension of credit, other than under an open-end credit plan (as defined in section 103(i)), in the name of the consumer, or issuance of an additional card on an existing credit account requested by a consumer, or any increase in credit limit on an existing credit account requested by a consumer, except in accordance with subparagraph (B).

(B) LIMITATION ON USERS.—

(i) IN GENERAL.—No prospective user of a consumer report that includes an initial fraud alert or an active duty alert in accordance with this section may establish a new credit plan or extension of credit, other than under an open-end credit plan (as defined in section 103(i)), in the name of the consumer, or issue an additional card on an existing credit account requested by a consumer, or grant any increase in credit limit on an existing credit account requested by a consumer, unless the user utilizes reasonable policies and procedures to form a reasonable belief that the user knows the identity of the person making the request.

(ii) VERIFICATION.—If a consumer requesting the alert has specified a telephone number to be used for identity verification purposes, before authorizing any new credit plan or extension described in clause (i) in the name of such consumer, a user of such consumer report shall contact the consumer using that telephone number or take reasonable steps to verify the consumer's identity and confirm that the application for a new credit plan is not the result of identity theft.

(2) REQUIREMENTS FOR EXTENDED ALERTS.—

(A) NOTIFICATION.—Each extended alert under this section shall include information that provides all prospective users of a consumer report relating to a consumer with—

(i) notification that the consumer does not authorize the establishment of any new credit plan or extension of credit described in clause (i), other than under an open-end credit plan (as defined in section 103(i)), in the name of the consumer, or issuance of an additional card on an existing credit account requested by a consumer, or any increase in credit limit on an existing credit account requested by a consumer, except in accordance with subparagraph (B); and

(ii) a telephone number or other reasonable contact method designated by the consumer.

(B) LIMITATION ON USERS.—No prospective user of a consumer report or of a credit score generated using the information in the file of a consumer that includes an extended fraud alert in accordance with this section may establish a new credit plan or extension of credit, other than under an open-end credit plan (as defined in section 103(i)), in the name of the consumer, or issue an additional card on an existing credit account requested by a consumer, or any increase in credit limit on an existing credit account requested by a consumer, unless the user contacts the consumer in person or using the contact method described in subparagraph (A)(ii) to confirm that the application for a new credit plan or increase in credit limit, or request for an additional card is not the result of identity theft.

(i) NATIONAL SECURITY FREEZE.—

(1) DEFINITIONS.—For purposes of this subsection:

(A) The term "consumer reporting agency" means a consumer reporting agency described in section 603(p).

(B) The term "proper identification" has the meaning of such term as used under section 610.

(C) The term "security freeze" means a restriction that prohibits a consumer reporting agency from disclosing the contents of a consumer report that is subject to such security freeze to any person requesting the consumer report.

(2) PLACEMENT OF SECURITY FREEZE.—

(A) IN GENERAL.—Upon receiving a direct request from a consumer that a consumer reporting agency place a security freeze, and upon receiving proper identification from the consumer, the consumer reporting agency shall, free of charge, place the security freeze not later than—
(i) in the case of a request that is by toll-free telephone or secure electronic means, 1 business day after receiving the request directly from the consumer; or
(ii) in the case of a request that is by mail, 3 business days after receiving the request directly from the consumer.
(B) CONFIRMATION AND ADDITIONAL INFORMATION.—Not later than 5 business days after placing a security freeze under subparagraph (A), a consumer reporting agency shall—
(i) send confirmation of the placement to the consumer; and
(ii) inform the consumer of—
(I) the process by which the consumer may remove the security freeze, including a mechanism to authenticate the consumer; and
(II) the consumer's right described in section 615(d)(1)(D).
(C) NOTICE TO THIRD PARTIES.—A consumer reporting agency may advise a third party that a security freeze has been placed with respect to a consumer under subparagraph (A).
(3) REMOVAL OF SECURITY FREEZE.—
(A) IN GENERAL.—A consumer reporting agency shall remove a security freeze placed on the consumer report of a consumer only in the following cases:
(i) Upon the direct request of the consumer.
(ii) The security freeze was placed due to a material misrepresentation of fact by the consumer.
(B) NOTICE IF REMOVAL NOT BY REQUEST.—If a consumer reporting agency removes a security freeze under subparagraph (A)(ii), the consumer reporting agency shall notify the consumer in writing prior to removing the security freeze.
(C) REMOVAL OF SECURITY FREEZE BY CONSUMER REQUEST.—Except as provided in subparagraph (A)(ii), a security freeze shall remain in place until the consumer directly requests that the security freeze be removed. Upon receiving a direct request from a consumer that a consumer reporting agency remove a security freeze, and upon receiving proper identification from the consumer, the consumer reporting agency shall, free of charge, remove the security freeze not later than—
(i) in the case of a request that is by toll-free telephone or secure electronic means, 1 hour after receiving the request for removal; or
(ii) in the case of a request that is by mail, 3 business days after receiving the request for removal.

(D) THIRD-PARTY REQUESTS.—If a third party requests access to a consumer report of a consumer with respect to which a security freeze is in effect, where such request is in connection with an application for credit, and the consumer does not allow such consumer report to be accessed, the third party may treat the application as incomplete.

(E) TEMPORARY REMOVAL OF SECURITY FREEZE.—Upon receiving a direct request from a consumer under subparagraph (A)(i), if the consumer requests a temporary removal of a security freeze, the consumer reporting agency shall, in accordance with subparagraph (C), remove the security freeze for the period of time specified by the consumer.

(4) EXCEPTIONS.—A security freeze shall not apply to the making of a consumer report for use of the following:

(A) A person or entity, or a subsidiary, affiliate, or agent of that person or entity, or an assignee of a financial obligation owed by the consumer to that person or entity, or a prospective assignee of a financial obligation owed by the consumer to that person or entity in conjunction with the proposed purchase of the financial obligation, with which the consumer has or had prior to assignment an account or contract including a demand deposit account, or to whom the consumer issued a negotiable instrument, for the purposes of reviewing the account or collecting the financial obligation owed for the account, contract, or negotiable instrument. For purposes of this subparagraph, "reviewing the account" includes activities related to account maintenance, monitoring, credit line increases, and account upgrades and enhancements.

(B) Any Federal, State, or local agency, law enforcement agency, trial court, or private collection agency acting pursuant to a court order, warrant, or subpoena.

(C) A child support agency acting pursuant to part D of title IV of the Social Security Act (42 U.S.C. 651 et seq.).

(D) A Federal agency or a State or its agents or assigns acting to investigate fraud or acting to investigate or collect delinquent taxes or unpaid court orders or to fulfill any of its other statutory responsibilities, provided such responsibilities are consistent with a permissible purpose under section 604.

(E) By a person using credit information for the purposes described under section 604(c).

(F) Any person or entity administering a credit file monitoring subscription or similar service to which the consumer has subscribed.

(G) Any person or entity for the purpose of providing a consumer with a copy of the consumer's consumer report or credit score, upon the request of the consumer.

(H) Any person using the information in connection with the underwriting of insurance.

(I) Any person using the information for employment, tenant, or background screening purposes.

(J) Any person using the information for assessing, verifying, or authenticating a consumer's identity for purposes other than the granting of credit, or for investigating or preventing actual or potential fraud.

(5) NOTICE OF RIGHTS.—At any time a consumer is required to receive a summary of rights required under section 609, the following notice shall be included:

"CONSUMERS HAVE THE RIGHT TO OBTAIN A SECURITY FREEZE

" 'You have a right to place a 'security freeze' on your credit report, which will prohibit a consumer reporting agency from releasing information in your credit report without your express authorization. The security freeze is designed to prevent credit, loans, and services from being approved in your name without your consent. However, you should be aware that using a security freeze to take control over who gets access to the personal and financial information in your credit report may delay, interfere with, or prohibit the timely approval of any subsequent request or application you make regarding a new loan, credit, mortgage, or any other account involving the extension of credit.'

" 'As an alternative to a security freeze, you have the right to place an initial or extended fraud alert on your credit file at no cost. An initial fraud alert is a 1-year alert that is placed on a consumer's credit file. Upon seeing a fraud alert display on a consumer's credit file, a business is required to take steps to verify the consumer's identity before extending new credit. If you are a victim of identity theft, you are entitled to an extended fraud alert, which is a fraud alert lasting 7 years.'

" 'A security freeze does not apply to a person or entity, or its affiliates, or collection agencies acting on behalf of the person or entity, with which you have an existing account that requests information in your credit report for the purposes of reviewing or collecting the account. Reviewing the account includes activities related to account maintenance, monitoring, credit line increases, and account upgrades and enhancements.'".

(6) WEBPAGE.—

(A) CONSUMER REPORTING AGENCIES.—A consumer reporting agency shall establish a webpage that—

(i) allows a consumer to request a security freeze;

(ii) allows a consumer to request an initial fraud alert;

(iii) allows a consumer to request an extended fraud alert;

(iv) allows a consumer to request an active duty fraud alert;

(v) allows a consumer to opt-out of the use of information in a consumer report to send the consumer a solicitation of credit or insurance, in accordance with section 615(d); and

(vi) shall not be the only mechanism by which a consumer may request a security freeze.

(B) FTC.—The Federal Trade Commission shall establish a single webpage that includes a link to each webpage established under subparagraph (A) within the Federal Trade Commission's website www.Identitytheft.gov, or a successor website.

(j) NATIONAL PROTECTION FOR FILES AND CREDIT RECORDS OF PROTECTED CONSUMERS.—

(1) DEFINITIONS.—As used in this subsection:

(A) The term "consumer reporting agency" means a consumer reporting agency described in section 603(p).

(B) The term "protected consumer" means an individual who is—

(i) under the age of 16 years at the time a request for the placement of a security freeze is made; or

(ii) an incapacitated person or a protected person for whom a guardian or conservator has been appointed.

(C) The term "protected consumer's representative" means a person who provides to a consumer reporting agency sufficient proof of authority to act on behalf of a protected consumer.

(D) The term "record" means a compilation of information that—

(i) identifies a protected consumer;

(ii) is created by a consumer reporting agency solely for the purpose of complying with this subsection; and

(iii) may not be created or used to consider the protected consumer's credit worthiness, credit standing, credit capacity, character, general reputation, personal characteristics, or mode of living.

(E) The term "security freeze" means a restriction that prohibits a consumer reporting agency from disclosing the contents of a consumer report that is the subject of such security freeze or, in the case of a protected consumer for whom the consumer reporting agency does not have a file, a record that is subject to such security freeze to any person requesting the consumer report for the purpose of opening a new account involving the extension of credit.

(F) The term "sufficient proof of authority" means documentation that shows a protected consumer's representative has authority to act on behalf of a protected consumer and includes—

(i) an order issued by a court of law;

(ii) a lawfully executed and valid power of attorney;

(iii) a document issued by a Federal, State, or local government agency in the United States showing proof of parentage, including a birth certificate; or

(iv) with respect to a protected consumer who has been placed in a foster care setting, a written communication from a county welfare department or its agent or designee, or a county probation department or its agent or designee, certifying that the protected consumer is in a foster care setting under its jurisdiction.

(G) The term "sufficient proof of identification" means information or documentation that identifies a protected consumer and a protected consumer's representative and includes—

(i) a social security number or a copy of a social security card issued by the Social Security Administration;

(ii) a certified or official copy of a birth certificate issued by the entity authorized to issue the birth certificate; or

(iii) a copy of a driver's license, an identification card issued by the motor vehicle administration, or any other government issued identification.

(2) PLACEMENT OF SECURITY FREEZE FOR A PROTECTED CONSUMER.—

(A) IN GENERAL.—Upon receiving a direct request from a protected consumer's representative that a consumer reporting agency place a security freeze, and upon receiving sufficient proof of identification and sufficient proof of authority, the consumer reporting agency shall, free of charge, place the security freeze not later than—

(i) in the case of a request that is by toll-free telephone or secure electronic means, 1 business day after receiving the request directly from the protected consumer's representative; or

(ii) in the case of a request that is by mail, 3 business days after receiving the request directly from the protected consumer's representative.

(B) CONFIRMATION AND ADDITIONAL INFORMATION.—Not later than 5 business days after placing a security freeze under subparagraph (A), a consumer reporting agency shall—

(i) send confirmation of the placement to the protected consumer's representative; and

(ii) inform the protected consumer's representative of the process by which the protected consumer may remove the security freeze, including a mechanism to authenticate the protected consumer's representative.

(C) CREATION OF FILE.—If a consumer reporting agency does not have a file pertaining to a protected consumer when the consumer reporting agency receives a direct request under subparagraph (A), the consumer reporting agency shall create a record for the protected consumer.

(3) PROHIBITION ON RELEASE OF RECORD OR FILE OF PROTECTED CONSUMER.—After a security freeze has been placed under paragraph (2)(A), and unless the security freeze is removed in accordance with this subsection, a consumer reporting agency may not release the protected consumer's consumer report, any information derived from the protected consumer's consumer report, or any record created for the protected consumer.

(4) REMOVAL OF A PROTECTED CONSUMER SECURITY FREEZE.—

(A) IN GENERAL.—A consumer reporting agency shall remove a security freeze placed on the consumer report of a protected consumer only in the following cases:

(i) Upon the direct request of the protected consumer's representative.

(ii) Upon the direct request of the protected consumer, if the protected consumer is not under the age of 16 years at the time of the request.

(iii) The security freeze was placed due to a material misrepresentation of fact by the protected consumer's representative.

(B) NOTICE IF REMOVAL NOT BY REQUEST.—If a consumer reporting agency removes a security freeze under subparagraph (A)(iii), the consumer reporting agency shall notify the protected consumer's representative in writing prior to removing the security freeze.

(C) REMOVAL OF FREEZE BY REQUEST.—Except as provided in subparagraph (A)(iii), a security freeze shall remain in place until a protected consumer's representative or protected consumer described in subparagraph (A)(ii) directly requests that the security freeze be removed. Upon receiving a direct request from the protected consumer's representative or protected consumer described in subparagraph (A)(ii) that a consumer reporting agency remove a security freeze, and upon receiving sufficient proof of identification and sufficient proof of authority, the consumer reporting agency shall, free of charge, remove the security freeze not later than—

(i) in the case of a request that is by toll-free telephone or secure electronic means, 1 hour after receiving the request for removal; or

(ii) in the case of a request that is by mail, 3 business days after receiving the request for removal.

(D) TEMPORARY REMOVAL OF SECURITY FREEZE.—Upon receiving a direct request from a protected consumer or a protected consumer's representative under subparagraph (A)(i), if the protected consumer or protected consumer's representative requests a temporary removal of a security freeze, the consumer reporting agency shall, in accordance with subparagraph (C), remove the security freeze for the period of time specified by the protected consumer or protected consumer's representative.

(k) CREDIT MONITORING.—

(1) DEFINITIONS.—In this subsection:

(A) The term "active duty military consumer" includes a member of the National Guard.

(B) The term "National Guard" has the meaning given the term in section 101(c) of title 10, United States Code.

(2) CREDIT MONITORING.—A consumer reporting agency described in section 603(p) shall provide a free electronic credit monitoring service that, at a minimum, notifies a consumer of material additions or modifications to the file of the consumer at the consumer reporting agency to any consumer who provides to the consumer reporting agency—

(A) appropriate proof that the consumer is an active duty military consumer; and

(B) contact information of the consumer.

(3) RULEMAKING.—Not later than 1 year after the date of enactment of this subsection, the Federal Trade Commission

shall promulgate regulations regarding the requirements of this subsection, which shall at a minimum include—

(A) a definition of an electronic credit monitoring service and material additions or modifications to the file of a consumer; and

(B) what constitutes appropriate proof.

(4) APPLICABILITY.—

(A) Sections 616 and 617 shall not apply to any violation of this subsection.

(B) This subsection shall be enforced exclusively under section 621 by the Federal agencies and Federal and State officials identified in that section.

§ 605B. [15 U.S.C. 1681c–2] Block of information resulting from identity theft

(a) BLOCK.—Except as otherwise provided in this section, a consumer reporting agency shall block the reporting of any information in the file of a consumer that the consumer identifies as information that resulted from an alleged identity theft, not later than 4 business days after the date of receipt by such agency of—

(1) appropriate proof of the identity of the consumer;

(2) a copy of an identity theft report;

(3) the identification of such information by the consumer; and

(4) a statement by the consumer that the information is not information relating to any transaction by the consumer.

(b) NOTIFICATION.—A consumer reporting agency shall promptly notify the furnisher of information identified by the consumer under subsection (a)—

(1) that the information may be a result of identity theft;

(2) that an identity theft report has been filed;

(3) that a block has been requested under this section; and

(4) of the effective dates of the block.

(c) AUTHORITY TO DECLINE OR RESCIND.—

(1) IN GENERAL.—A consumer reporting agency may decline to block, or may rescind any block, of information relating to a consumer under this section, if the consumer reporting agency reasonably determines that—

(A) the information was blocked in error or a block was requested by the consumer in error;

(B) the information was blocked, or a block was requested by the consumer, on the basis of a material misrepresentation of fact by the consumer relevant to the request to block; or

(C) the consumer obtained possession of goods, services, or money as a result of the blocked transaction or transactions.

(2) NOTIFICATION TO CONSUMER.—If a block of information is declined or rescinded under this subsection, the affected consumer shall be notified promptly, in the same manner as consumers are notified of the reinsertion of information under section 611(a)(5)(B).

(3) SIGNIFICANCE OF BLOCK.—For purposes of this subsection, if a consumer reporting agency rescinds a block, the

presence of information in the file of a consumer prior to the blocking of such information is not evidence of whether the consumer knew or should have known that the consumer obtained possession of any goods, services, or money as a result of the block.

(d) EXCEPTION FOR RESELLERS.—

(1) NO RESELLER FILE.—This section shall not apply to a consumer reporting agency, if the consumer reporting agency—

(A) is a reseller;

(B) is not, at the time of the request of the consumer under subsection (a), otherwise furnishing or reselling a consumer report concerning the information identified by the consumer; and

(C) informs the consumer, by any means, that the consumer may report the identity theft to the Bureau to obtain consumer information regarding identity theft.

(2) RESELLER WITH FILE.—The sole obligation of the consumer reporting agency under this section, with regard to any request of a consumer under this section, shall be to block the consumer report maintained by the consumer reporting agency from any subsequent use, if—

(A) the consumer, in accordance with the provisions of subsection (a), identifies, to a consumer reporting agency, information in the file of the consumer that resulted from identity theft; and

(B) the consumer reporting agency is a reseller of the identified information.

(3) NOTICE.—In carrying out its obligation under paragraph (2), the reseller shall promptly provide a notice to the consumer of the decision to block the file. Such notice shall contain the name, address, and telephone number of each consumer reporting agency from which the consumer information was obtained for resale.

(e) EXCEPTION FOR VERIFICATION COMPANIES.—The provisions of this section do not apply to a check services company, acting as such, which issues authorizations for the purpose of approving or processing negotiable instruments, electronic fund transfers, or similar methods of payments, except that, beginning 4 business days after receipt of information described in paragraphs (1) through (3) of subsection (a), a check services company shall not report to a national consumer reporting agency described in section 603(p), any information identified in the subject identity theft report as resulting from identity theft.

(f) ACCESS TO BLOCKED INFORMATION BY LAW ENFORCEMENT AGENCIES.—No provision of this section shall be construed as requiring a consumer reporting agency to prevent a Federal, State, or local law enforcement agency from accessing blocked information in a consumer file to which the agency could otherwise obtain access under this title.

§ 606. [15 U.S.C. 1681d] Disclosure of investigative consumer reports

(a) A person may not procure or cause to be prepared an investigative consumer report on any consumer unless—

(1) it is clearly and accurately disclosed to the consumer that an investigative consumer report including information as to his character, general reputation, personal characteristics, and mode of living, whichever are applicable, may be made, and such disclosure (A) is made in a writing mailed, or otherwise delivered, to the consumer, not later than three days after the date on which the report was first requested, and (B) includes a statement informing the consumer of his right to request the additional disclosures provided for under subsection (b) of this section and the written summary of the rights of the consumer prepared pursuant to section 609(c); and

(2) the person certifies or has certified to the consumer reporting agency that—

    (A) the person has made the disclosures to the consumer required by paragraph (1); and

    (B) the person will comply with subsection (b).

(b) Any person who procures or causes to be prepared an investigative consumer report on any consumer shall, upon written request made by the consumer within a reasonable period of time after the receipt by him of the disclosure required by subsection (a)(1), make a complete and accurate disclosure of the nature and scope of the investigation requested. This disclosure shall be made in a writing mailed, or otherwise delivered, to the consumer not later than five days after the date on which the request for such disclosure was received from the consumer or such report was first requested, whichever is the later.

(c) No person may be held liable for any violation of subsection (a) or (b) of this section if he shows by a preponderance of the evidence that at the time of the violation he maintained reasonable procedures to assure compliance with subsection (a) or (b).

(d) PROHIBITIONS.—

(1) CERTIFICATION.—A consumer reporting agency shall not prepare or furnish an investigative consumer report unless the agency has received a certification under subsection (a)(2) from the person who requested the report.

(2) INQUIRIES.—A consumer reporting agency shall not make an inquiry for the purpose of preparing an investigative consumer report on a consumer for employment purposes if the making of the inquiry by an employer or prospective employer of the consumer would violate any applicable Federal or State equal employment opportunity law or regulation.

(3) CERTAIN PUBLIC RECORD INFORMATION.—Except as otherwise provided in section 613, a consumer reporting agency shall not furnish an investigative consumer report that includes information that is a matter of public record and that relates to an arrest, indictment, conviction, civil judicial action, tax lien, or outstanding judgment, unless the agency has verified the accuracy of the information during the 30-day period ending on the date on which the report is furnished.

(4) CERTAIN ADVERSE INFORMATION.—A consumer reporting agency shall not prepare or furnish an investigative consumer report on a consumer that contains information that is adverse to the interest of the consumer and that is obtained through a personal interview with a neighbor, friend, or asso-

ciate of the consumer or with another person with whom the consumer is acquainted or who has knowledge of such item of information, unless—

(A) the agency has followed reasonable procedures to obtain confirmation of the information, from an additional source that has independent and direct knowledge of the information; or

(B) the person interviewed is the best possible source of the information.

§ 607. [15 U.S.C. 1681e] Compliance procedures

(a) Every consumer reporting agency shall maintain reasonable procedures designed to avoid violations of section 605 and to limit the furnishing of consumer reports to the purposes listed under section 604. These procedures shall require that prospective users of the information identify themselves, certify the purposes for which the information is sought, and certify that the information will be used for no other purpose. Every consumer reporting agency shall make a reasonable effort to verify the identity of a new prospective user and the uses certified by such prospective user prior to furnishing such user a consumer report. No consumer reporting agency may furnish a consumer report to any person if it has reasonable grounds for believing that the consumer report will not be used for a purpose listed in section 604.

(b) Whenever a consumer reporting agency prepares a consumer report it shall follow reasonable procedures to assure maximum possible accuracy of the information concerning the individual about whom the report relates.

(c) DISCLOSURE OF CONSUMER REPORTS BY USERS ALLOWED.— A consumer reporting agency may not prohibit a user of a consumer report furnished by the agency on a consumer from disclosing the contents of the report to the consumer, if adverse action against the consumer has been taken by the user based in whole or in part on the report.

(d) NOTICE TO USERS AND FURNISHERS OF INFORMATION.—

(1) NOTICE REQUIREMENT.—A consumer reporting agency shall provide to any person—

(A) who regularly and in the ordinary course of business furnishes information to the agency with respect to any consumer; or

(B) to whom a consumer report is provided by the agency;

a notice of such person's responsibilities under this title.

(2) CONTENT OF NOTICE.—The Bureau shall prescribe the content of notices under paragraph (1), and a consumer reporting agency shall be in compliance with this subsection if it provides a notice under paragraph (1) that is substantially similar to the Bureau prescription under this paragraph.

(e) PROCUREMENT OF CONSUMER REPORT FOR RESALE.—

(1) DISCLOSURE.—A person may not procure a consumer report for purposes of reselling the report (or any information in the report) unless the person discloses to the consumer reporting agency that originally furnishes the report—

(A) the identity of the end-user of the report (or information); and

(B) each permissible purpose under section 604 for which the report is furnished to the end-user of the report (or information).

(2) RESPONSIBILITIES OF PROCURERS FOR RESALE.—A person who procures a consumer report for purposes of reselling the report (or any information in the report) shall—

(A) establish and comply with reasonable procedures designed to ensure that the report (or information) is resold by the person only for a purpose for which the report may be furnished under section 604, including by requiring that each person to which the report (or information) is resold and that resells or provides the report (or information) to any other person—

(i) identifies each end user of the resold report (or information);

(ii) certifies each purpose for which the report (or information) will be used; and

(iii) certifies that the report (or information) will be used for no other purpose; and

(B) before reselling the report, make reasonable efforts to verify the identifications and certifications made under subparagraph (A).

(3) RESALE OF CONSUMER REPORT TO A FEDERAL AGENCY OR DEPARTMENT.—Notwithstanding paragraph (1) or (2), a person who procures a consumer report for purposes of reselling the report (or any information in the report) shall not disclose the identity of the end-user of the report under paragraph (1) or (2) if—

(A) the end user is an agency or department of the United States Government which procures the report from the person for purposes of determining the eligibility of the consumer concerned to receive access or continued access to classified information (as defined in section 604(b)(4)(E)(i)); and

(B) the agency or department certifies in writing to the person reselling the report that nondisclosure is necessary to protect classified information or the safety of persons employed by or contracting with, or undergoing investigation for work or contracting with the agency or department.

§ 608. [15 U.S.C. 1681f] Disclosures to governmental agencies

Notwithstanding the provisions of section 604, a consumer reporting agency may furnish identifying information respecting any consumer, limited to his name, address, former addresses, places of employment, or former places of employment, to a governmental agency.

§ 609. [15 U.S.C. 1681g] Disclosures to consumers

(a) Every consumer reporting agency shall, upon request, and subject to section 610(a)(1), clearly and accurately disclose to the consumer:

(1) All information in the consumer's file at the time of the request, except that—

(A) if the consumer to whom the file relates requests that the first 5 digits of the social security number (or similar identification number) of the consumer not be included in the disclosure and the consumer reporting agency has received appropriate proof of the identity of the requester, the consumer reporting agency shall so truncate such number in such disclosure; and

(B) nothing in this paragraph shall be construed to require a consumer reporting agency to disclose to a consumer any information concerning credit scores or any other risk scores or predictors relating to the consumer.

(2) The sources of the information; except that the sources of information acquired solely for use in preparing an investigative consumer report and actually used for no other purpose need not be disclosed: *Provided,* That in the event an action is brought under this title, such sources shall be available to the plaintiff under appropriate discovery procedures in the court in which the action is brought.

(3)(A) Identification of each person (including each end-user identified under section 607(e)(1)) that procured a consumer report—

(i) for employment purposes, during the 2-year period preceding the date on which the request is made; or

(ii) for any other purpose, during the 1-year period preceding the date on which the request is made.

(B) An identification of a person under subparagraph (A) shall include—

(i) the name of the person or, if applicable, the trade name (written in full) under which such person conducts business; and

(ii) upon request of the consumer, the address and telephone number of the person.

(C) Subparagraph (A) does not apply if—

(i) the end user is an agency or department of the United States Government that procures the report from the person for purposes of determining the eligibility of the consumer to whom the report relates to receive access or continued access to classified information (as defined in section 604(b)(4)(E)(i)); and

(ii) the head of the agency or department makes a written finding as prescribed under section 604(b)(4)(A).

(4) The dates, original payees, and amounts of any checks upon which is based any adverse characterization of the consumer, included in the file at the time of the disclosure.

(5) A record of all inquiries received by the agency during the 1-year period preceding the request that identified the consumer in connection with a credit or insurance transaction that was not initiated by the consumer.

(6) If the consumer requests the credit file and not the credit score, a statement that the consumer may request and obtain a credit score.

(b) The requirements of subsection (a) respecting the disclosure of sources of information and the recipients of consumer reports do not apply to information received or consumer reports furnished prior to the effective date of this title except to the extent that the matter involved is contained in the files of the consumer reporting agency on that date.

(c) SUMMARY OF RIGHTS TO OBTAIN AND DISPUTE INFORMATION IN CONSUMER REPORTS AND TO OBTAIN CREDIT SCORES.—

(1) COMMISSION SUMMARY OF RIGHTS REQUIRED.—

(A) IN GENERAL.—The Commission shall prepare a model summary of the rights of consumers under this title.

(B) CONTENT OF SUMMARY.—The summary of rights prepared under subparagraph (A) shall include a description of—

(i) the right of a consumer to obtain a copy of a consumer report under subsection (a) from each consumer reporting agency;

(ii) the frequency and circumstances under which a consumer is entitled to receive a consumer report without charge under section 612;

(iii) the right of a consumer to dispute information in the file of the consumer under section 611;

(iv) the right of a consumer to obtain a credit score from a consumer reporting agency, and a description of how to obtain a credit score;

(v) the method by which a consumer can contact, and obtain a consumer report from, a consumer reporting agency without charge, as provided in the regulations of the Bureau prescribed under section 211(c) of the Fair and Accurate Credit Transactions Act of 2003; and

(vi) the method by which a consumer can contact, and obtain a consumer report from, a consumer reporting agency described in section 603(w), as provided in the regulations of the Bureau prescribed under section 612(a)(1)(C).

(C) AVAILABILITY OF SUMMARY OF RIGHTS.—The Commission shall—

(i) actively publicize the availability of the summary of rights prepared under this paragraph;

(ii) conspicuously post on its Internet website the availability of such summary of rights; and

(iii) promptly make such summary of rights available to consumers, on request.

(2) SUMMARY OF RIGHTS REQUIRED TO BE INCLUDED WITH AGENCY DISCLOSURES.—A consumer reporting agency shall provide to a consumer, with each written disclosure by the agency to the consumer under this section—

(A) the summary of rights prepared by the Bureau under paragraph (1);

(B) in the case of a consumer reporting agency described in section 603(p), a toll-free telephone number established by the agency, at which personnel are accessible to consumers during normal business hours;

(C) a list of all Federal agencies responsible for enforcing any provision of this title, and the address and any appropriate phone number of each such agency, in a form that will assist the consumer in selecting the appropriate agency;

(D) a statement that the consumer may have additional rights under State law, and that the consumer may wish to contact a State or local consumer protection agency or a State attorney general (or the equivalent thereof) to learn of those rights; and

(E) a statement that a consumer reporting agency is not required to remove accurate derogatory information from the file of a consumer, unless the information is outdated under section 605 or cannot be verified.

(d) SUMMARY OF RIGHTS OF IDENTITY THEFT VICTIMS.—

(1) IN GENERAL.—The Commission, in consultation with the Federal banking agencies and the National Credit Union Administration, shall prepare a model summary of the rights of consumers under this title with respect to the procedures for remedying the effects of fraud or identity theft involving credit, an electronic fund transfer, or an account or transaction at or with a financial institution or other creditor.

(2) SUMMARY OF RIGHTS AND CONTACT INFORMATION.—Beginning 60 days after the date on which the model summary of rights is prescribed in final form by the Bureau pursuant to paragraph (1), if any consumer contacts a consumer reporting agency and expresses a belief that the consumer is a victim of fraud or identity theft involving credit, an electronic fund transfer, or an account or transaction at or with a financial institution or other creditor, the consumer reporting agency shall, in addition to any other action that the agency may take, provide the consumer with a summary of rights that contains all of the information required by the Bureau under paragraph (1), and information on how to contact the Bureau to obtain more detailed information.

(e) INFORMATION AVAILABLE TO VICTIMS.—

(1) IN GENERAL.—For the purpose of documenting fraudulent transactions resulting from identity theft, not later than 30 days after the date of receipt of a request from a victim in accordance with paragraph (3), and subject to verification of the identity of the victim and the claim of identity theft in accordance with paragraph (2), a business entity that has provided credit to, provided for consideration products, goods, or services to, accepted payment from, or otherwise entered into a commercial transaction for consideration with, a person who has allegedly made unauthorized use of the means of identification of the victim, shall provide a copy of application and business transaction records in the control of the business entity, whether maintained by the business entity or by another person on behalf of the business entity, evidencing any transaction alleged to be a result of identity theft to—

(A) the victim;

(B) any Federal, State, or local government law enforcement agency or officer specified by the victim in such a request; or

(C) any law enforcement agency investigating the identity theft and authorized by the victim to take receipt of records provided under this subsection.

(2) VERIFICATION OF IDENTITY AND CLAIM.—Before a business entity provides any information under paragraph (1), unless the business entity, at its discretion, otherwise has a high degree of confidence that it knows the identity of the victim making a request under paragraph (1), the victim shall provide to the business entity—

(A) as proof of positive identification of the victim, at the election of the business entity—

(i) the presentation of a government-issued identification card;

(ii) personally identifying information of the same type as was provided to the business entity by the unauthorized person; or

(iii) personally identifying information that the business entity typically requests from new applicants or for new transactions, at the time of the victim's request for information, including any documentation described in clauses (i) and (ii); and

(B) as proof of a claim of identity theft, at the election of the business entity—

(i) a copy of a police report evidencing the claim of the victim of identity theft; and

(ii) a properly completed—

(I) copy of a standardized affidavit of identity theft developed and made available by the Bureau; or

(II) an affidavit of fact that is acceptable to the business entity for that purpose.

(3) PROCEDURES.—The request of a victim under paragraph (1) shall—

(A) be in writing;

(B) be mailed to an address specified by the business entity, if any; and

(C) if asked by the business entity, include relevant information about any transaction alleged to be a result of identity theft to facilitate compliance with this section including—

(i) if known by the victim (or if readily obtainable by the victim), the date of the application or transaction; and

(ii) if known by the victim (or if readily obtainable by the victim), any other identifying information such as an account or transaction number.

(4) NO CHARGE TO VICTIM.—Information required to be provided under paragraph (1) shall be so provided without charge.

(5) AUTHORITY TO DECLINE TO PROVIDE INFORMATION.—A business entity may decline to provide information under para-

graph (1) if, in the exercise of good faith, the business entity determines that—

(A) this subsection does not require disclosure of the information;

(B) after reviewing the information provided pursuant to paragraph (2), the business entity does not have a high degree of confidence in knowing the true identity of the individual requesting the information;

(C) the request for the information is based on a misrepresentation of fact by the individual requesting the information relevant to the request for information; or

(D) the information requested is Internet navigational data or similar information about a person's visit to a website or online service.

(6) LIMITATION ON LIABILITY.—Except as provided in section 621, sections 616 and 617 do not apply to any violation of this subsection.

(7) LIMITATION ON CIVIL LIABILITY.—No business entity may be held civilly liable under any provision of Federal, State, or other law for disclosure, made in good faith pursuant to this subsection.

(8) NO NEW RECORDKEEPING OBLIGATION.—Nothing in this subsection creates an obligation on the part of a business entity to obtain, retain, or maintain information or records that are not otherwise required to be obtained, retained, or maintained in the ordinary course of its business or under other applicable law.

(9) RULE OF CONSTRUCTION.—

(A) IN GENERAL.—No provision of subtitle A of title V of Public Law 106–102, prohibiting the disclosure of financial information by a business entity to third parties shall be used to deny disclosure of information to the victim under this subsection.

(B) LIMITATION.—Except as provided in subparagraph (A), nothing in this subsection permits a business entity to disclose information, including information to law enforcement under subparagraphs (B) and (C) of paragraph (1), that the business entity is otherwise prohibited from disclosing under any other applicable provision of Federal or State law.

(10) AFFIRMATIVE DEFENSE.—In any civil action brought to enforce this subsection, it is an affirmative defense (which the defendant must establish by a preponderance of the evidence) for a business entity to file an affidavit or answer stating that—

(A) the business entity has made a reasonably diligent search of its available business records; and

(B) the records requested under this subsection do not exist or are not reasonably available.

(11) DEFINITION OF VICTIM.—For purposes of this subsection, the term "victim" means a consumer whose means of identification or financial information has been used or transferred (or has been alleged to have been used or transferred)

without the authority of that consumer, with the intent to commit, or to aid or abet, an identity theft or a similar crime.

(12) EFFECTIVE DATE.—This subsection shall become effective 180 days after the date of enactment of this subsection.

(13) EFFECTIVENESS STUDY.—Not later than 18 months after the date of enactment of this subsection, the Comptroller General of the United States shall submit a report to Congress assessing the effectiveness of this provision.

(f) DISCLOSURE OF CREDIT SCORES.—

(1) IN GENERAL.—Upon the request of a consumer for a credit score, a consumer reporting agency shall supply to the consumer a statement indicating that the information and credit scoring model may be different than the credit score that may be used by the lender, and a notice which shall include—

(A) the current credit score of the consumer or the most recent credit score of the consumer that was previously calculated by the credit reporting agency for a purpose related to the extension of credit;

(B) the range of possible credit scores under the model used;

(C) all of the key factors that adversely affected the credit score of the consumer in the model used, the total number of which shall not exceed 4, subject to paragraph (9);

(D) the date on which the credit score was created; and

(E) the name of the person or entity that provided the credit score or credit file upon which the credit score was created.

(2) DEFINITIONS.—For purposes of this subsection, the following definitions shall apply:

(A) CREDIT SCORE.—The term "credit score"—

(i) means a numerical value or a categorization derived from a statistical tool or modeling system used by a person who makes or arranges a loan to predict the likelihood of certain credit behaviors, including default (and the numerical value or the categorization derived from such analysis may also be referred to as a "risk predictor" or "risk score"); and

(ii) does not include—

(I) any mortgage score or rating of an automated underwriting system that considers one or more factors in addition to credit information, including the loan to value ratio, the amount of down payment, or the financial assets of a consumer; or

(II) any other elements of the underwriting process or underwriting decision.

(B) KEY FACTORS.—The term "key factors" means all relevant elements or reasons adversely affecting the credit score for the particular individual, listed in the order of their importance based on their effect on the credit score.

(3) TIMEFRAME AND MANNER OF DISCLOSURE.—The information required by this subsection shall be provided in the

same timeframe and manner as the information described in subsection (a).

(4) APPLICABILITY TO CERTAIN USES.—This subsection shall not be construed so as to compel a consumer reporting agency to develop or disclose a score if the agency does not—

(A) distribute scores that are used in connection with residential real property loans; or

(B) develop scores that assist credit providers in understanding the general credit behavior of a consumer and predicting the future credit behavior of the consumer.

(5) APPLICABILITY TO CREDIT SCORES DEVELOPED BY ANOTHER PERSON.—

(A) IN GENERAL.—This subsection shall not be construed to require a consumer reporting agency that distributes credit scores developed by another person or entity to provide a further explanation of them, or to process a dispute arising pursuant to section 611, except that the consumer reporting agency shall provide the consumer with the name and address and website for contacting the person or entity who developed the score or developed the methodology of the score.

(B) EXCEPTION.—This paragraph shall not apply to a consumer reporting agency that develops or modifies scores that are developed by another person or entity.

(6) MAINTENANCE OF CREDIT SCORES NOT REQUIRED.—This subsection shall not be construed to require a consumer reporting agency to maintain credit scores in its files.

(7) COMPLIANCE IN CERTAIN CASES.—In complying with this subsection, a consumer reporting agency shall—

(A) supply the consumer with a credit score that is derived from a credit scoring model that is widely distributed to users by that consumer reporting agency in connection with residential real property loans or with a credit score that assists the consumer in understanding the credit scoring assessment of the credit behavior of the consumer and predictions about the future credit behavior of the consumer; and

(B) a statement indicating that the information and credit scoring model may be different than that used by the lender.

(8) FAIR AND REASONABLE FEE.—A consumer reporting agency may charge a fair and reasonable fee, as determined by the Bureau, for providing the information required under this subsection.

(9) USE OF ENQUIRIES AS A KEY FACTOR.—If a key factor that adversely affects the credit score of a consumer consists of the number of enquiries made with respect to a consumer report, that factor shall be included in the disclosure pursuant to paragraph (1)(C) without regard to the numerical limitation in such paragraph.

(g) DISCLOSURE OF CREDIT SCORES BY CERTAIN MORTGAGE LENDERS.—

(1) IN GENERAL.—Any person who makes or arranges loans and who uses a consumer credit score, as defined in subsection

(f), in connection with an application initiated or sought by a consumer for a closed end loan or the establishment of an open end loan for a consumer purpose that is secured by 1 to 4 units of residential real property (hereafter in this subsection referred to as the "lender") shall provide the following to the consumer as soon as reasonably practicable:

(A) INFORMATION REQUIRED UNDER SUBSECTION (f).—

(i) IN GENERAL.—A copy of the information identified in subsection (f) that was obtained from a consumer reporting agency or was developed and used by the user of the information.

(ii) NOTICE UNDER SUBPARAGRAPH (D).—In addition to the information provided to it by a third party that provided the credit score or scores, a lender is only required to provide the notice contained in subparagraph (D).

(B) DISCLOSURES IN CASE OF AUTOMATED UNDERWRITING SYSTEM.—

(i) IN GENERAL.—If a person that is subject to this subsection uses an automated underwriting system to underwrite a loan, that person may satisfy the obligation to provide a credit score by disclosing a credit score and associated key factors supplied by a consumer reporting agency.

(ii) NUMERICAL CREDIT SCORE.—However, if a numerical credit score is generated by an automated underwriting system used by an enterprise, and that score is disclosed to the person, the score shall be disclosed to the consumer consistent with subparagraph (C).

(iii) ENTERPRISE DEFINED.—For purposes of this subparagraph, the term "enterprise" has the same meaning as in paragraph (6) of section 1303 of the Federal Housing Enterprises Financial Safety and Soundness Act of 1992.

(C) DISCLOSURES OF CREDIT SCORES NOT OBTAINED FROM A CONSUMER REPORTING AGENCY.—A person that is subject to the provisions of this subsection and that uses a credit score, other than a credit score provided by a consumer reporting agency, may satisfy the obligation to provide a credit score by disclosing a credit score and associated key factors supplied by a consumer reporting agency.

(D) NOTICE TO HOME LOAN APPLICANTS.—A copy of the following notice, which shall include the name, address, and telephone number of each consumer reporting agency providing a credit score that was used:

"NOTICE TO THE HOME LOAN APPLICANT

"In connection with your application for a home loan, the lender must disclose to you the score that a consumer reporting agency distributed to users and the lender used in connection with your home loan, and the key factors affecting your credit scores.

"The credit score is a computer generated summary calculated at the time of the request and based on information that a consumer reporting agency or lender has on file. The scores are based on data about your credit history and payment patterns. Credit scores are important because they are used to assist the lender in determining whether you will obtain a loan. They may also be used to determine what interest rate you may be offered on the mortgage. Credit scores can change over time, depending on your conduct, how your credit history and payment patterns change, and how credit scoring technologies change.

"Because the score is based on information in your credit history, it is very important that you review the credit-related information that is being furnished to make sure it is accurate. Credit records may vary from one company to another.

"If you have questions about your credit score or the credit information that is furnished to you, contact the consumer reporting agency at the address and telephone number provided with this notice, or contact the lender, if the lender developed or generated the credit score. The consumer reporting agency plays no part in the decision to take any action on the loan application and is unable to provide you with specific reasons for the decision on a loan application.

"If you have questions concerning the terms of the loan, contact the lender.".

(E) ACTIONS NOT REQUIRED UNDER THIS SUBSECTION.—This subsection shall not require any person to—

(i) explain the information provided pursuant to subsection (f);

(ii) disclose any information other than a credit score or key factors, as defined in subsection (f);

(iii) disclose any credit score or related information obtained by the user after a loan has closed;

(iv) provide more than 1 disclosure per loan transaction; or

(v) provide the disclosure required by this subsection when another person has made the disclosure to the consumer for that loan transaction.

(F) NO OBLIGATION FOR CONTENT.—

(i) IN GENERAL.—The obligation of any person pursuant to this subsection shall be limited solely to providing a copy of the information that was received from the consumer reporting agency.

(ii) LIMIT ON LIABILITY.—No person has liability under this subsection for the content of that information or for the omission of any information within the report provided by the consumer reporting agency.

(G) PERSON DEFINED AS EXCLUDING ENTERPRISE.—As used in this subsection, the term "person" does not include an enterprise (as defined in paragraph (6) of section 1303 of the Federal Housing Enterprises Financial Safety and Soundness Act of 1992).

(2) PROHIBITION ON DISCLOSURE CLAUSES NULL AND VOID.—

(A) IN GENERAL.—Any provision in a contract that prohibits the disclosure of a credit score by a person who makes or arranges loans or a consumer reporting agency is void.

(B) NO LIABILITY FOR DISCLOSURE UNDER THIS SUBSECTION.—A lender shall not have liability under any contractual provision for disclosure of a credit score pursuant to this subsection.

§ 610. [15 U.S.C. 1681h] Conditions and form of disclosure to consumers

(a) IN GENERAL.—

(1) PROPER IDENTIFICATION.—A consumer reporting agency shall require, as a condition of making the disclosures required under section 609, that the consumer furnish proper identification.

(2) DISCLOSURE IN WRITING.—Except as provided in subsection (b), the disclosures required to be made under section 609 shall be provided under that section in writing.

(b) OTHER FORMS OF DISCLOSURE.—

(1) IN GENERAL.—If authorized by a consumer, a consumer reporting agency may make the disclosures required under 609—

(A) other than in writing; and

(B) in such form as may be—

(i) specified by the consumer in accordance with paragraph (2); and

(ii) available from the agency.

(2) FORM.—A consumer may specify pursuant to paragraph (1) that disclosures under section 609 shall be made—

(A) in person, upon the appearance of the consumer at the place of business of the consumer reporting agency where disclosures are regularly provided, during normal business hours, and on reasonable notice;

(B) by telephone, if the consumer has made a written request for disclosure by telephone;

(C) by electronic means, if available from the agency; or

(D) by any other reasonable means that is available from the agency.

(c) Any consumer reporting agency shall provide trained personnel to explain to the consumer any information furnished to him pursuant to section 609.

(d) The consumer shall be permitted to be accompanied by one other person of his choosing, who shall furnish reasonable identification. A consumer reporting agency may require the consumer to furnish a written statement granting permission to the consumer reporting agency to discuss the consumer's file in such person's presence.

(e) Except as provided in sections 616 and 617, no consumer may bring any action or proceeding in the nature of defamation, invasion of privacy, or negligence with respect to the reporting of information against any consumer reporting agency, any user of information, or any person who furnishes information to a consumer reporting agency, based on information disclosed pursuant to section 609, 610, or 615, or based on information disclosed by a user of a consumer report to or for a consumer against whom the user has taken adverse action, based in whole or in part on the report except as to false information furnished with malice or willful intent to injure such consumer.

§ 611. [15 U.S.C. 1681i] Procedure in case of disputed accuracy

(a) REINVESTIGATIONS OF DISPUTED INFORMATION.—

(1) REINVESTIGATION REQUIRED.—

(A) IN GENERAL.—Subject to subsection (f) and except as provided in subsection (g), if the completeness or accuracy of any item of information contained in a consumer's file at a consumer reporting agency is disputed by the consumer and the consumer notifies the agency directly, or indirectly through a reseller, of such dispute, the agency shall, free of charge, conduct a reasonable reinvestigation to determine whether the disputed information is inaccurate and record the current status of the disputed information, or delete the item from the file in accordance with paragraph (5), before the end of the 30-day period beginning on the date on which the agency receives the notice of the dispute from the consumer or reseller.

(B) EXTENSION OF PERIOD TO REINVESTIGATE.—Except as provided in subparagraph (C), the 30-day period described in subparagraph (A) may be extended for not more than 15 additional days if the consumer reporting agency receives information from the consumer during that 30-day period that is relevant to the reinvestigation.

(C) LIMITATIONS ON EXTENSION OF PERIOD TO REINVESTIGATE.—Subparagraph (B) shall not apply to any reinvestigation in which, during the 30-day period described in subparagraph (A), the information that is the subject of the reinvestigation is found to be inaccurate or incomplete or the consumer reporting agency determines that the information cannot be verified.

(2) PROMPT NOTICE OF DISPUTE TO FURNISHER OF INFORMATION.—

(A) IN GENERAL.—Before the expiration of the 5-business-day period beginning on the date on which a consumer reporting agency receives notice of a dispute from any consumer or a reseller in accordance with paragraph (1), the agency shall provide notification of the dispute to any person who provided any item of information in dispute, at the address and in the manner established with the person. The notice shall include all relevant information regarding the dispute that the agency has received from the consumer or reseller.

(B) PROVISION OF OTHER INFORMATION.—The consumer reporting agency shall promptly provide to the person who provided the information in dispute all relevant information regarding the dispute that is received by the agency from the consumer or the reseller after the period referred to in subparagraph (A) and before the end of the period referred to in paragraph (1)(A).

(3) DETERMINATION THAT DISPUTE IS FRIVOLOUS OR IRRELEVANT.—

(A) IN GENERAL.—Notwithstanding paragraph (1), a consumer reporting agency may terminate a reinvestigation of information disputed by a consumer under that paragraph if the agency reasonably determines that the dispute by the consumer is frivolous or irrelevant, including by reason of a failure by a consumer to provide sufficient information to investigate the disputed information.

(B) NOTICE OF DETERMINATION.—Upon making any determination in accordance with subparagraph (A) that a dispute is frivolous or irrelevant, a consumer reporting agency shall notify the consumer of such determination not later than 5 business days after making such determination, by mail or, if authorized by the consumer for that purpose, by any other means available to the agency.

(C) CONTENTS OF NOTICE.—A notice under subparagraph (B) shall include—

(i) the reasons for the determination under subparagraph (A); and

(ii) identification of any information required to investigate the disputed information, which may consist of a standardized form describing the general nature of such information.

(4) CONSIDERATION OF CONSUMER INFORMATION.—In conducting any reinvestigation under paragraph (1) with respect to disputed information in the file of any consumer, the consumer reporting agency shall review and consider all relevant information submitted by the consumer in the period described in paragraph (1)(A) with respect to such disputed information.

(5) TREATMENT OF INACCURATE OR UNVERIFIABLE INFORMATION.—

(A) IN GENERAL.—If, after any reinvestigation under paragraph (1) of any information disputed by a consumer, an item of the information is found to be inaccurate or incomplete or cannot be verified, the consumer reporting agency shall—

(i) promptly delete that item of information from the file of the consumer, or modify that item of information, as appropriate, based on the results of the reinvestigation; and

(ii) promptly notify the furnisher of that information that the information has been modified or deleted from the file of the consumer.

(B) REQUIREMENTS RELATING TO REINSERTION OF PREVIOUSLY DELETED MATERIAL.—

(i) CERTIFICATION OF ACCURACY OF INFORMATION.—If any information is deleted from a consumer's file pursuant to subparagraph (A), the information may not be reinserted in the file by the consumer reporting agency unless the person who furnishes the information certifies that the information is complete and accurate.

(ii) NOTICE TO CONSUMER.—If any information that has been deleted from a consumer's file pursuant to subparagraph (A) is reinserted in the file, the consumer reporting agency shall notify the consumer of the reinsertion in writing not later than 5 business days after the reinsertion or, if authorized by the consumer for that purpose, by any other means available to the agency.

(iii) ADDITIONAL INFORMATION.—As part of, or in addition to, the notice under clause (ii), a consumer reporting agency shall provide to a consumer in writing not later than 5 business days after the date of the reinsertion—

(I) a statement that the disputed information has been reinserted;

(II) the business name and address of any furnisher of information contacted and the telephone number of such furnisher, if reasonably available, or of any furnisher of information that contacted the consumer reporting agency, in connection with the reinsertion of such information; and

(III) a notice that the consumer has the right to add a statement to the consumer's file disputing the accuracy or completeness of the disputed information.

(C) PROCEDURES TO PREVENT REAPPEARANCE.—A consumer reporting agency shall maintain reasonable procedures designed to prevent the reappearance in a consumer's file, and in consumer reports on the consumer, of information that is deleted pursuant to this paragraph (other than information that is reinserted in accordance with subparagraph (B)(i)).

(D) AUTOMATED REINVESTIGATION SYSTEM.—Any consumer reporting agency that compiles and maintains files on consumers on a nationwide basis shall implement an automated system through which furnishers of information to that consumer reporting agency may report the results of a reinvestigation that finds incomplete or inaccurate information in a consumer's file to other such consumer reporting agencies.

(6) NOTICE OF RESULTS OF REINVESTIGATION.—

(A) IN GENERAL.—A consumer reporting agency shall provide written notice to a consumer of the results of a reinvestigation under this subsection not later than 5 business days after the completion of the reinvestigation, by mail or, if authorized by the consumer for that purpose, by other means available to the agency.

(B) CONTENTS.—As part of, or in addition to, the notice under subparagraph (A), a consumer reporting agency shall provide to a consumer in writing before the expiration of the 5-day period referred to in subparagraph (A)—

(i) a statement that the reinvestigation is completed;

(ii) a consumer report that is based upon the consumer's file as that file is revised as a result of the reinvestigation;

(iii) a notice that, if requested by the consumer, a description of the procedure used to determine the accuracy and completeness of the information shall be provided to the consumer by the agency, including the business name and address of any furnisher of information contacted in connection with such information and the telephone number of such furnisher, if reasonably available;

(iv) a notice that the consumer has the right to add a statement to the consumer's file disputing the accuracy or completeness of the information; and

(v) a notice that the consumer has the right to request under subsection (d) that the consumer reporting agency furnish notifications under that subsection.

(7) DESCRIPTION OF REINVESTIGATION PROCEDURE.—A consumer reporting agency shall provide to a consumer a description referred to in paragraph (6)(B)(iii) by not later than 15 days after receiving a request from the consumer for that description.

(8) EXPEDITED DISPUTE RESOLUTION.—If a dispute regarding an item of information in a consumer's file at a consumer reporting agency is resolved in accordance with paragraph (5)(A) by the deletion of the disputed information by not later than 3 business days after the date on which the agency receives notice of the dispute from the consumer in accordance with paragraph (1)(A), then the agency shall not be required to comply with paragraphs (2), (6), and (7) with respect to that dispute if the agency—

(A) provides prompt notice of the deletion to the consumer by telephone;

(B) includes in that notice, or in a written notice that accompanies a confirmation and consumer report provided in accordance with subparagraph (C), a statement of the consumer's right to request under subsection (d) that the agency furnish notifications under that subsection; and

(C) provides written confirmation of the deletion and a copy of a consumer report on the consumer that is based on the consumer's file after the deletion, not later than 5 business days after making the deletion.

(b) If the reinvestigation does not resolve the dispute, the consumer may file a brief statement setting forth the nature of the dispute. The consumer reporting agency may limit such statements to not more than one hundred words if it provides the consumer with assistance in writing a clear summary of the dispute.

(c) Whenever a statement of a dispute is filed, unless there is reasonable grounds to believe that it is frivolous or irrelevant, the consumer reporting agency shall, in any subsequent consumer report containing the information in question, clearly note that it is disputed by the consumer and provide either the consumer's statement or a clear and accurate codification or summary thereof.

FAIR CREDIT REPORTING ACT Sec. 611

(d) Following any deletion of information which is found to be inaccurate or whose accuracy can no longer be verified or any notation as to disputed information, the consumer reporting agency shall, at the request of the consumer, furnish notification that the item has been deleted or the statement, codification or summary pursuant to subsection (b) or (c) to any person specifically designated by the consumer who has within two years prior thereto received a consumer report for employment purposes, or within six months prior thereto received a consumer report for any other purpose, which contained the deleted or disputed information.

(e) TREATMENT OF COMPLAINTS AND REPORT TO CONGRESS.—

(1) IN GENERAL.—The Commission shall—

(A) compile all complaints that it receives that a file of a consumer that is maintained by a consumer reporting agency described in section 603(p) contains incomplete or inaccurate information, with respect to which, the consumer appears to have disputed the completeness or accuracy with the consumer reporting agency or otherwise utilized the procedures provided by subsection (a); and

(B) transmit each such complaint to each consumer reporting agency involved.

(2) EXCLUSION.—Complaints received or obtained by the Bureau pursuant to its investigative authority under the Consumer Financial Protection Act of 2010 shall not be subject to paragraph (1).

(3) AGENCY RESPONSIBILITIES.—Each consumer reporting agency described in section 603(p) that receives a complaint transmitted by the Bureau pursuant to paragraph (1) shall—

(A) review each such complaint to determine whether all legal obligations imposed on the consumer reporting agency under this title (including any obligation imposed by an applicable court or administrative order) have been met with respect to the subject matter of the complaint;

(B) provide reports on a regular basis to the Bureau regarding the determinations of and actions taken by the consumer reporting agency, if any, in connection with its review of such complaints; and

(C) maintain, for a reasonable time period, records regarding the disposition of each such complaint that is sufficient to demonstrate compliance with this subsection. (4) RULEMAKING AUTHORITY.—The Bureau [3] may prescribe regulations, as appropriate to implement this subsection.

(5) ANNUAL REPORT.—The Bureau [3] shall submit to the Committee on Banking, Housing, and Urban Affairs of the Senate and the Committee on Financial Services of the House of Representatives an annual report regarding information gathered by the Bureau under this subsection.

(f) REINVESTIGATION REQUIREMENT APPLICABLE TO RESELLERS.—

---

[3] Amendment made to strike "the Commission" and insert "the Bureau" by section 1088(a)(2)(C) of Public Law 111–203 was executed by striking "[T]he Commission" and inserting "[T]he Bureau" in order to reflect the probable intent of Congress.

(1) EXEMPTION FROM GENERAL REINVESTIGATION REQUIREMENT.—Except as provided in paragraph (2), a reseller shall be exempt from the requirements of this section.

(2) ACTION REQUIRED UPON RECEIVING NOTICE OF A DISPUTE.—If a reseller receives a notice from a consumer of a dispute concerning the completeness or accuracy of any item of information contained in a consumer report on such consumer produced by the reseller, the reseller shall, within 5 business days of receiving the notice, and free of charge—

(A) determine whether the item of information is incomplete or inaccurate as a result of an act or omission of the reseller; and

(B) if—

(i) the reseller determines that the item of information is incomplete or inaccurate as a result of an act or omission of the reseller, not later than 20 days after receiving the notice, correct the information in the consumer report or delete it; or

(ii) if the reseller determines that the item of information is not incomplete or inaccurate as a result of an act or omission of the reseller, convey the notice of the dispute, together with all relevant information provided by the consumer, to each consumer reporting agency that provided the reseller with the information that is the subject of the dispute, using an address or a notification mechanism specified by the consumer reporting agency for such notices.

(3) RESPONSIBILITY OF CONSUMER REPORTING AGENCY TO NOTIFY CONSUMER THROUGH RESELLER.—Upon the completion of a reinvestigation under this section of a dispute concerning the completeness or accuracy of any information in the file of a consumer by a consumer reporting agency that received notice of the dispute from a reseller under paragraph (2)—

(A) the notice by the consumer reporting agency under paragraph (6), (7), or (8) of subsection (a) shall be provided to the reseller in lieu of the consumer; and

(B) the reseller shall immediately reconvey such notice to the consumer, including any notice of a deletion by telephone in the manner required under paragraph (8)(A).

(4) RESELLER REINVESTIGATIONS.—No provision of this subsection shall be construed as prohibiting a reseller from conducting a reinvestigation of a consumer dispute directly.

(g) DISPUTE PROCESS FOR VETERAN'S MEDICAL DEBT.—

(1) IN GENERAL.—With respect to a veteran's medical debt, the veteran may submit a notice described in paragraph (2), proof of liability of the Department of Veterans Affairs for payment of that debt, or documentation that the Department of Veterans Affairs is in the process of making payment for authorized hospital care, medical services, or extended care services rendered to a consumer reporting agency or a reseller to dispute the inclusion of that debt on a consumer report of the veteran.

(2) NOTIFICATION TO VETERAN.—The Department of Veterans Affairs shall submit to a veteran a notice that the De-

partment of Veterans Affairs has assumed liability for part or all of a veteran's medical debt.

(3) DELETION OF INFORMATION FROM FILE.—If a consumer reporting agency receives notice, proof of liability, or documentation under paragraph (1), the consumer reporting agency shall delete all information relating to the veteran's medical debt from the file of the veteran and notify the furnisher and the veteran of that deletion.

SEC. 612. [15 U.S.C. 1681j] CHARGES FOR CERTAIN DISCLOSURES.

(a) FREE ANNUAL DISCLOSURE.—
  (1) NATIONWIDE CONSUMER REPORTING AGENCIES.—
    (A) IN GENERAL.—All consumer reporting agencies described in subsections (p) and (w) of section 603 shall make all disclosures pursuant to section 609 once during any 12-month period upon request of the consumer and without charge to the consumer.
    (B) CENTRALIZED SOURCE.—Subparagraph (A) shall apply with respect to a consumer reporting agency described in section 603(p) only if the request from the consumer is made using the centralized source established for such purpose in accordance with section 211(c) of the Fair and Accurate Credit Transactions Act of 2003.
    (C) NATIONWIDE SPECIALTY CONSUMER REPORTING AGENCY.—
      (i) IN GENERAL.—The Commission shall prescribe regulations applicable to each consumer reporting agency described in section 603(w) to require the establishment of a streamlined process for consumers to request consumer reports under subparagraph (A), which shall include, at a minimum, the establishment by each such agency of a toll-free telephone number for such requests.
      (ii) CONSIDERATIONS.—In prescribing regulations under clause (i), the Bureau shall consider—
        (I) the significant demands that may be placed on consumer reporting agencies in providing such consumer reports;
        (II) appropriate means to ensure that consumer reporting agencies can satisfactorily meet those demands, including the efficacy of a system of staggering the availability to consumers of such consumer reports; and
        (III) the ease by which consumers should be able to contact consumer reporting agencies with respect to access to such consumer reports.
      (iii) DATE OF ISSUANCE.—The Commission shall issue the regulations required by this subparagraph in final form not later than 6 months after the date of enactment of the Fair and Accurate Credit Transactions Act of 2003.
      (iv) CONSIDERATION OF ABILITY TO COMPLY.—The regulations of the Bureau under this subparagraph shall establish an effective date by which each nation-

wide specialty consumer reporting agency (as defined in section 603(w)) shall be required to comply with subsection (a), which effective date—
 (I) shall be established after consideration of the ability of each nationwide specialty consumer reporting agency to comply with subsection (a); and
 (II) shall be not later than 6 months after the date on which such regulations are issued in final form (or such additional period not to exceed 3 months, as the Bureau determines appropriate).

(2) TIMING.—A consumer reporting agency shall provide a consumer report under paragraph (1) not later than 15 days after the date on which the request is received under paragraph (1).

(3) REINVESTIGATIONS.—Notwithstanding the time periods specified in section 611(a)(1), a reinvestigation under that section by a consumer reporting agency upon a request of a consumer that is made after receiving a consumer report under this subsection shall be completed not later than 45 days after the date on which the request is received.

(4) EXCEPTION FOR FIRST 12 MONTHS OF OPERATION.—This subsection shall not apply to a consumer reporting agency that has not been furnishing consumer reports to third parties on a continuing basis during the 12-month period preceding a request under paragraph (1), with respect to consumers residing nationwide.

(b) FREE DISCLOSURE AFTER ADVERSE NOTICE TO CONSUMER.—Each consumer reporting agency that maintains a file on a consumer shall make all disclosures pursuant to section 609 without charge to the consumer if, not later than 60 days after receipt by such consumer of a notification pursuant to section 615, or of a notification from a debt collection agency affiliated with that consumer reporting agency stating that the consumer's credit rating may be or has been adversely affected, the consumer makes a request under section 609.

(c) FREE DISCLOSURE UNDER CERTAIN OTHER CIRCUMSTANCES.—Upon the request of the consumer, a consumer reporting agency shall make all disclosures pursuant to section 609 once during any 12-month period without charge to that consumer if the consumer certifies in writing that the consumer—
 (1) is unemployed and intends to apply for employment in the 60-day period beginning on the date on which the certification is made;
 (2) is a recipient of public welfare assistance; or
 (3) has reason to believe that the file on the consumer at the agency contains inaccurate information due to fraud.

(d) FREE DISCLOSURES IN CONNECTION WITH FRAUD ALERTS.—Upon the request of a consumer, a consumer reporting agency described in section 603(p) shall make all disclosures pursuant to section 609 without charge to the consumer, as provided in subsections (a)(2) and (b)(2) of section 605A, as applicable.

(e) OTHER CHARGES PROHIBITED.—A consumer reporting agency shall not impose any charge on a consumer for providing any notification required by this title or making any disclosure required by this title, except as authorized by subsection (f).

(f) REASONABLE CHARGES ALLOWED FOR CERTAIN DISCLOSURES.—

(1) IN GENERAL.—In the case of a request from a consumer other than a request that is covered by any of subsections (a) through (d), a consumer reporting agency may impose a reasonable charge on a consumer—

(A) for making a disclosure to the consumer pursuant to section 609, which charge—

(i) shall not exceed $8; and

(ii) shall be indicated to the consumer before making the disclosure; and

(B) for furnishing, pursuant to section 611(d), following a reinvestigation under section 611(a), a statement, codification, or summary to a person designated by the consumer under that section after the 30-day period beginning on the date of notification of the consumer under paragraph (6) or (8) of section 611(a) with respect to the reinvestigation, which charge—

(i) shall not exceed the charge that the agency would impose on each designated recipient for a consumer report; and

(ii) shall be indicated to the consumer before furnishing such information.

(2) MODIFICATION OF AMOUNT.—The Bureau shall increase the amount referred to in paragraph (1)(A)(i) on January 1 of each year, based proportionally on changes in the Consumer Price Index, with fractional changes rounded to the nearest fifty cents.

(g) PREVENTION OF DECEPTIVE MARKETING OF CREDIT REPORTS.—

(1) IN GENERAL.—Subject to rulemaking pursuant to section 205(b) of the Credit CARD Act of 2009, any advertisement for a free credit report in any medium shall prominently disclose in such advertisement that free credit reports are available under Federal law at: "AnnualCreditReport.com" (or such other source as may be authorized under Federal law).

(2) TELEVISION AND RADIO ADVERTISEMENT.—In the case of an advertisement broadcast by television, the disclosures required under paragraph (1) shall be included in the audio and visual part of such advertisement. In the case of an advertisement broadcast by televison [4] or radio, the disclosure required under paragraph (1) shall consist only of the following: "This is not the free credit report provided for by Federal law".

§ 613. [15 U.S.C. 1681k] Public record information for employment purposes

(a) IN GENERAL.—A consumer reporting agency which furnishes a consumer report for employment purposes and which for that purpose compiles and reports items of information on consumers which are matters of public record and are likely to have

---

[4] So in law. Probably should read "television".

an adverse effect upon a consumer's ability to obtain employment shall—

(1) at the time such public record information is reported to the user of such consumer report, notify the consumer of the fact that public record information is being reported by the consumer reporting agency, together with the name and address of the person to whom such information is being reported; or

(2) maintain strict procedures designed to insure that whenever public record information which is likely to have an adverse effect on a consumer's ability to obtain employment is reported it is complete and up to date. For purposes of this paragraph, items of public record relating to arrests, indictments, convictions, suits, tax liens, and outstanding judgments shall be considered up to date if the current public record status of the item at the time of the report is reported.

(b) EXEMPTION FOR NATIONAL SECURITY INVESTIGATIONS.—Subsection (a) does not apply in the case of an agency or department of the United States Government that seeks to obtain and use a consumer report for employment purposes, if the head of the agency or department makes a written finding as prescribed under section 604(b)(4)(A).

§ 614. [15 U.S.C. 1681*l*] Restrictions on investigative consumer reports

Whenever a consumer reporting agency prepares an investigative consumer report, no adverse information in the consumer report (other than information which is a matter of public record) may be included in a subsequent consumer report unless such adverse information has been verified in the process of making such subsequent consumer report, or the adverse information was received within the three-month period preceding the date the subsequent report is furnished.

§ 615. [15 U.S.C. 1681m] Requirements on users of consumer reports

(a) DUTIES OF USERS TAKING ADVERSE ACTIONS ON THE BASIS OF INFORMATION CONTAINED IN CONSUMER REPORTS.—If any person takes any adverse action with respect to any consumer that is based in whole or in part on any information contained in a consumer report, the person shall—

(1) provide oral, written, or electronic notice of the adverse action to the consumer;

(2) provide to the consumer written or electronic disclosure—

(A) of a numerical credit score as defined in section 609(f)(2)(A) used by such person in taking any adverse action based in whole or in part on any information in a consumer report; and

(B) of the information set forth in subparagraphs (B) through (E) of section 609(f)(1);

(3) provide to the consumer orally, in writing, or electronically—

(A) the name, address, and telephone number of the consumer reporting agency (including a toll-free telephone number established by the agency if the agency compiles and maintains files on consumers on a nationwide basis) that furnished the report to the person; and

(B) a statement that the consumer reporting agency did not make the decision to take the adverse action and is unable to provide the consumer the specific reasons why the adverse action was taken; and

(4) provide to the consumer an oral, written, or electronic notice of the consumer's right—

(A) to obtain, under section 612, a free copy of a consumer report on the consumer from the consumer reporting agency referred to in paragraph (3), which notice shall include an indication of the 60-day period under that section for obtaining such a copy; and

(B) to dispute, under section 611, with a consumer reporting agency the accuracy or completeness of any information in a consumer report furnished by the agency.

(b) ADVERSE ACTION BASED ON INFORMATION OBTAINED FROM THIRD PARTIES OTHER THAN CONSUMER REPORTING AGENCIES.—

(1) IN GENERAL.—Whenever credit for personal, family, or household purposes involving a consumer is denied or the charge for such credit is increased either wholly or partly because of information obtained from a person other than a consumer reporting agency bearing upon the consumer's credit worthiness, credit standing, credit capacity, character, general reputation, personal characteristics, or mode of living, the user of such information shall, within a reasonable period of time, upon the consumer's written request for the reasons for such adverse action received within sixty days after learning of such adverse action, disclose the nature of the information to the consumer. The user of such information shall clearly and accurately disclose to the consumer his right to make such written request at the time such adverse action is communicated to the consumer.

(2) DUTIES OF PERSON TAKING CERTAIN ACTIONS BASED ON INFORMATION PROVIDED BY AFFILIATE.—

(A) DUTIES, GENERALLY.—If a person takes an action described in subparagraph (B) with respect to a consumer, based in whole or in part on information described in subparagraph (C), the person shall—

(i) notify the consumer of the action, including a statement that the consumer may obtain the information in accordance with clause (ii); and

(ii) upon a written request from the consumer received within 60 days after transmittal of the notice required by clause (i), disclose to the consumer the nature of the information upon which the action is based by not later than 30 days after receipt of the request.

(B) ACTION DESCRIBED.—An action referred to in subparagraph (A) is an adverse action described in section 603(k)(1)(A), taken in connection with a transaction initiated by the consumer, or any adverse action described in clause (i) or (ii) of section 603(k)(1)(B).

(C) INFORMATION DESCRIBED.—Information referred to in subparagraph (A)—

(i) except as provided in clause (ii), is information that—

(I) is furnished to the person taking the action by a person related by common ownership or affiliated by common corporate control to the person taking the action; and

(II) bears on the credit worthiness, credit standing, credit capacity, character, general reputation, personal characteristics, or mode of living of the consumer; and

(ii) does not include—

(I) information solely as to transactions or experiences between the consumer and the person furnishing the information; or

(II) information in a consumer report.

(c) No person shall be held liable for any violation of this section if he shows by a preponderance of the evidence that at the time of the alleged violation he maintained reasonable procedures to assure compliance with the provisions of this section.

(d) DUTIES OF USERS MAKING WRITTEN CREDIT OR INSURANCE SOLICITATIONS ON THE BASIS OF INFORMATION CONTAINED IN CONSUMER FILES.—

(1) IN GENERAL.—Any person who uses a consumer report on any consumer in connection with any credit or insurance transaction that is not initiated by the consumer, that is provided to that person under section 604(c)(1)(B), shall provide with each written solicitation made to the consumer regarding the transaction a clear and conspicuous statement that—

(A) information contained in the consumer's consumer report was used in connection with the transaction;

(B) the consumer received the offer of credit or insurance because the consumer satisfied the criteria for credit worthiness or insurability under which the consumer was selected for the offer;

(C) if applicable, the credit or insurance may not be extended if, after the consumer responds to the offer, the consumer does not meet the criteria used to select the consumer for the offer or any applicable criteria bearing on credit worthiness or insurability or does not furnish any required collateral;

(D) the consumer has a right to prohibit information contained in the consumer's file with any consumer reporting agency from being used in connection with any credit or insurance transaction that is not initiated by the consumer; and

(E) the consumer may exercise the right referred to in subparagraph (D) by notifying a notification system established under section 604(e).

(2) DISCLOSURE OF ADDRESS AND TELEPHONE NUMBER; FORMAT.—A statement under paragraph (1) shall—

(A) include the address and toll-free telephone number of the appropriate notification system established under section 604(e); and

(B) be presented in such format and in such type size and manner as to be simple and easy to understand, as established by the Bureau, by rule, in consultation with the Federal Trade Commission, the Federal banking agencies, and the National Credit Union Administration.

(3) MAINTAINING CRITERIA ON FILE.—A person who makes an offer of credit or insurance to a consumer under a credit or insurance transaction described in paragraph (1) shall maintain on file the criteria used to select the consumer to receive the offer, all criteria bearing on credit worthiness or insurability, as applicable, that are the basis for determining whether or not to extend credit or insurance pursuant to the offer, and any requirement for the furnishing of collateral as a condition of the extension of credit or insurance, until the expiration of the 3-year period beginning on the date on which the offer is made to the consumer.

(4) AUTHORITY OF FEDERAL AGENCIES REGARDING UNFAIR OR DECEPTIVE ACTS OR PRACTICES NOT AFFECTED.—This section is not intended to affect the authority of any Federal or State agency to enforce a prohibition against unfair or deceptive acts or practices, including the making of false or misleading statements in connection with a credit or insurance transaction that is not initiated by the consumer.

(e) RED FLAG GUIDELINES AND REGULATIONS REQUIRED.—

(1) GUIDELINES.—The Federal banking agencies, the National Credit Union Administration, the Federal Trade Commission, the Commodity Futures Trading Commission, and the Securities and Exchange Commission shall jointly, with respect to the entities that are subject to their respective enforcement authority under section 621—

(A) establish and maintain guidelines for use by each financial institution and each creditor regarding identity theft with respect to account holders at, or customers of, such entities, and update such guidelines as often as necessary;

(B) prescribe regulations requiring each financial institution and each creditor to establish reasonable policies and procedures for implementing the guidelines established pursuant to subparagraph (A), to identify possible risks to account holders or customers or to the safety and soundness of the institution or customers; and

(C) prescribe regulations applicable to card issuers to ensure that, if a card issuer receives notification of a change of address for an existing account, and within a short period of time (during at least the first 30 days after such notification is received) receives a request for an additional or replacement card for the same account, the card issuer may not issue the additional or replacement card, unless the card issuer, in accordance with reasonable policies and procedures—

(i) notifies the cardholder of the request at the former address of the cardholder and provides to the cardholder a means of promptly reporting incorrect address changes;

(ii) notifies the cardholder of the request by such other means of communication as the cardholder and the card issuer previously agreed to; or

(iii) uses other means of assessing the validity of the change of address, in accordance with reasonable policies and procedures established by the card issuer in accordance with the regulations prescribed under subparagraph (B).

(2) CRITERIA.—

(A) IN GENERAL.—In developing the guidelines required by paragraph (1)(A), the agencies described in paragraph (1) shall identify patterns, practices, and specific forms of activity that indicate the possible existence of identity theft.

(B) INACTIVE ACCOUNTS.—In developing the guidelines required by paragraph (1)(A), the agencies described in paragraph (1) shall consider including reasonable guidelines providing that when a transaction occurs with respect to a credit or deposit account that has been inactive for more than 2 years, the creditor or financial institution shall follow reasonable policies and procedures that provide for notice to be given to a consumer in a manner reasonably designed to reduce the likelihood of identity theft with respect to such account.

(3) CONSISTENCY WITH VERIFICATION REQUIREMENTS.—Guidelines established pursuant to paragraph (1) shall not be inconsistent with the policies and procedures required under section 5318(l) of title 31, United States Code.

(4) DEFINITIONS.—As used in this subsection, the term "creditor"—

(A) means a creditor, as defined in section 702 of the Equal Credit Opportunity Act (15 U.S.C. 1691a), that regularly and in the ordinary course of business—

(i) obtains or uses consumer reports, directly or indirectly, in connection with a credit transaction;

(ii) furnishes information to consumer reporting agencies, as described in section 623, in connection with a credit transaction; or

(iii) advances funds to or on behalf of a person, based on an obligation of the person to repay the funds or repayable from specific property pledged by or on behalf of the person;

(B) does not include a creditor described in subparagraph (A)(iii) that advances funds on behalf of a person for expenses incidental to a service provided by the creditor to that person; and

(C) includes any other type of creditor, as defined in that section 702, as the agency described in paragraph (1) having authority over that creditor may determine appropriate by rule promulgated by that agency, based on a determination that such creditor offers or maintains accounts that are subject to a reasonably foreseeable risk of identity theft.

(f) PROHIBITION ON SALE OR TRANSFER OF DEBT CAUSED BY IDENTITY THEFT.—

(1) IN GENERAL.—No person shall sell, transfer for consideration, or place for collection a debt that such person has been notified under section 605B has resulted from identity theft.

(2) APPLICABILITY.—The prohibitions of this subsection shall apply to all persons collecting a debt described in paragraph (1) after the date of a notification under paragraph (1).

(3) RULE OF CONSTRUCTION.—Nothing in this subsection shall be construed to prohibit—

(A) the repurchase of a debt in any case in which the assignee of the debt requires such repurchase because the debt has resulted from identity theft;

(B) the securitization of a debt or the pledging of a portfolio of debt as collateral in connection with a borrowing; or

(C) the transfer of debt as a result of a merger, acquisition, purchase and assumption transaction, or transfer of substantially all of the assets of an entity.

(g) DEBT COLLECTOR COMMUNICATIONS CONCERNING IDENTITY THEFT.—If a person acting as a debt collector (as that term is defined in title VIII) on behalf of a third party that is a creditor or other user of a consumer report is notified that any information relating to a debt that the person is attempting to collect may be fraudulent or may be the result of identity theft, that person shall—

(1) notify the third party that the information may be fraudulent or may be the result of identity theft; and

(2) upon request of the consumer to whom the debt purportedly relates, provide to the consumer all information to which the consumer would otherwise be entitled if the consumer were not a victim of identity theft, but wished to dispute the debt under provisions of law applicable to that person.

(h) DUTIES OF USERS IN CERTAIN CREDIT TRANSACTIONS.—

(1) IN GENERAL.—Subject to rules prescribed as provided in paragraph (6), if any person uses a consumer report in connection with an application for, or a grant, extension, or other provision of, credit on material terms that are materially less favorable than the most favorable terms available to a substantial proportion of consumers from or through that person, based in whole or in part on a consumer report, the person shall provide an oral, written, or electronic notice to the consumer in the form and manner required by regulations prescribed in accordance with this subsection.

(2) TIMING.—The notice required under paragraph (1) may be provided at the time of an application for, or a grant, extension, or other provision of, credit or the time of communication of an approval of an application for, or grant, extension, or other provision of, credit, except as provided in the regulations prescribed under paragraph (6).

(3) EXCEPTIONS.—No notice shall be required from a person under this subsection if—

(A) the consumer applied for specific material terms and was granted those terms, unless those terms were initially specified by the person after the transaction was initiated by the consumer and after the person obtained a consumer report; or

(B) the person has provided or will provide a notice to the consumer under subsection (a) in connection with the transaction.

(4) OTHER NOTICE NOT SUFFICIENT.—A person that is required to provide a notice under subsection (a) cannot meet that requirement by providing a notice under this subsection.

(5) CONTENT AND DELIVERY OF NOTICE.—A notice under this subsection shall, at a minimum—

(A) include a statement informing the consumer that the terms offered to the consumer are set based on information from a consumer report;

(B) identify the consumer reporting agency furnishing the report;

(C) include a statement informing the consumer that the consumer may obtain a copy of a consumer report from that consumer reporting agency without charge;

(D) include the contact information specified by that consumer reporting agency for obtaining such consumer reports (including a toll-free telephone number established by the agency in the case of a consumer reporting agency described in section 603(p)); and

(E) include a statement informing the consumer of—

(i) a numerical credit score as defined in section 609(f)(2)(A), used by such person in making the credit decision described in paragraph (1) based in whole or in part on any information in a consumer report; and

(ii) the information set forth in subparagraphs (B) through (E) of section 609(f)(1).

(6) RULEMAKING.—

(A) RULES REQUIRED.—The Bureau shall prescribe rules to carry out this subsection.

(B) CONTENT.—Rules required by subparagraph (A) shall address, but are not limited to—

(i) the form, content, time, and manner of delivery of any notice under this subsection;

(ii) clarification of the meaning of terms used in this subsection, including what credit terms are material, and when credit terms are materially less favorable;

(iii) exceptions to the notice requirement under this subsection for classes of persons or transactions regarding which the agencies determine that notice would not significantly benefit consumers;

(iv) a model notice that may be used to comply with this subsection; and

(v) the timing of the notice required under paragraph (1), including the circumstances under which the notice must be provided after the terms offered to the consumer were set based on information from a consumer report.

(7) COMPLIANCE.—A person shall not be liable for failure to perform the duties required by this section if, at the time of the failure, the person maintained reasonable policies and procedures to comply with this section.

(8) ENFORCEMENT.—

(A) NO CIVIL ACTIONS.—Sections 616 and 617 shall not apply to any failure by any person to comply with this section.

(B) ADMINISTRATIVE ENFORCEMENT.—This section shall be enforced exclusively under section 621 by the Federal agencies and officials identified in that section.

§ 616. [15 U.S.C. 1681n] Civil liability for willful noncompliance

(a) IN GENERAL.—Any person who willfully fails to comply with any requirement imposed under this title with respect to any consumer is liable to that consumer in an amount equal to the sum of—

(1)(A) any actual damages sustained by the consumer as a result of the failure or damages of not less than $100 and not more than $1,000; or

(B) in the case of liability of a natural person for obtaining a consumer report under false pretenses or knowingly without a permissible purpose, actual damages sustained by the consumer as a result of the failure or $1,000, whichever is greater;

(2) such amount of punitive damages as the court may allow; and

(3) in the case of any successful action to enforce any liability under this section, the costs of the action together with reasonable attorney's fees as determined by the court.

(b) CIVIL LIABILITY FOR KNOWING NONCOMPLIANCE.—Any person who obtains a consumer report from a consumer reporting agency under false pretenses or knowingly without a permissible purpose shall be liable to the consumer reporting agency for actual damages sustained by the consumer reporting agency or $1,000, whichever is greater.

(c) ATTORNEY'S FEES.—Upon a finding by the court that an unsuccessful pleading, motion, or other paper filed in connection with an action under this section was filed in bad faith or for purposes of harassment, the court shall award to the prevailing party attorney's fees reasonable in relation to the work expended in responding to the pleading, motion, or other paper.

(d) CLARIFICATION OF WILLFUL NONCOMPLIANCE.—For the purposes of this section, any person who printed an expiration date on any receipt provided to a consumer cardholder at a point of sale or transaction between December 4, 2004, and the date of the enactment of this subsection but otherwise complied with the requirements of section 605(g) for such receipt shall not be in willful noncompliance with section 605(g) by reason of printing such expiration date on the receipt.

§ 617. [15 U.S.C. 1681o] Civil liability for negligent noncompliance

(a) IN GENERAL.—Any person who is negligent in failing to comply with any requirement imposed under this title with respect to any consumer is liable to that consumer in an amount equal to the sum of—

(1) any actual damages sustained by the consumer as a result of the failure; and

(2) in the case of any successful action to enforce any liability under this section, the costs of the action together with reasonable attorney's fees as determined by the court.

(b) ATTORNEY'S FEES.—On a finding by the court that an unsuccessful pleading, motion, or other paper filed in connection with an action under this section was filed in bad faith or for purposes of harassment, the court shall award to the prevailing party attorney's fees reasonable in relation to the work expended in responding to the pleading, motion, or other paper.

§ 618. [15 U.S.C. 1681p] Jurisdiction of courts; limitation of actions

An action to enforce any liability created under this title may be brought in any appropriate United States district court, without regard to the amount in controversy, or in any other court of competent jurisdiction, not later than the earlier of—

(1) 2 years after the date of discovery by the plaintiff of the violation that is the basis for such liability; or

(2) 5 years after the date on which the violation that is the basis for such liability occurs.

§ 619. [15 U.S.C. 1681q] Obtaining information under false pretenses

Any person who knowingly and willfully obtains information on a consumer from a consumer reporting agency under false pretenses shall be fined under title 18, United States Code, imprisoned for not more than 2 years, or both.

§ 620. [15 U.S.C. 1681r] Unauthorized disclosures by officers or employees

Any officer or employee of a consumer reporting agency who knowingly and willfully provides information concerning an individual from the agency's files to a person not authorized to receive that information shall be fined under title 18, United States Code, imprisoned for not more than 2 years, or both.

§ 621. [15 U.S.C. 1681s] Administrative enforcement

(a) ENFORCEMENT BY FEDERAL TRADE COMMISSION.—

(1) IN GENERAL.—The Federal Trade Commission shall be authorized to enforce compliance with the requirements imposed by this title under the Federal Trade Commission Act (15 U.S.C. 41 et seq.), with respect to consumer reporting agencies and all other persons subject thereto, except to the extent that enforcement of the requirements imposed under this title is specifically committed to some other Government agency

under any of subparagraphs (A) through (G) of subsection (b)(1), and subject to subtitle B of the Consumer Financial Protection Act of 2010, subsection (b). For the purpose of the exercise by the Federal Trade Commission of its functions and powers under the Federal Trade Commission Act, a violation of any requirement or prohibition imposed under this title shall constitute an unfair or deceptive act or practice in commerce, in violation of section 5(a) of the Federal Trade Commission Act (15 U.S.C. 45(a)), and shall be subject to enforcement by the Federal Trade Commission under section 5(b) of that Act with respect to any consumer reporting agency or person that is subject to enforcement by the Federal Trade Commission pursuant to this subsection, irrespective of whether that person is engaged in commerce or meets any other jurisdictional tests under the Federal Trade Commission Act. The Federal Trade Commission shall have such procedural, investigative, and enforcement powers, including the power to issue procedural rules in enforcing compliance with the requirements imposed under this title and to require the filing of reports, the production of documents, and the appearance of witnesses, as though the applicable terms and conditions of the Federal Trade Commission Act were part of this title. Any person violating any of the provisions of this title shall be subject to the penalties and entitled to the privileges and immunities provided in the Federal Trade Commission Act as though the applicable terms and provisions of such Act are part of this title.

(2) PENALTIES.—

(A) KNOWING VIOLATIONS.—Except as otherwise provided by subtitle B of the Consumer Financial Protection Act of 2010, in the event of a knowing violation, which constitutes a pattern or practice of violations of this title, the Federal Trade Commission may commence a civil action to recover a civil penalty in a district court of the United States against any person that violates this title. In such action, such person shall be liable for a civil penalty of not more than $2,500 per violation.

(B) DETERMINING PENALTY AMOUNT.—In determining the amount of a civil penalty under subparagraph (A), the court shall take into account the degree of culpability, any history of such prior conduct, ability to pay, effect on ability to continue to do business, and such other matters as justice may require.

(C) LIMITATION.—Notwithstanding paragraph (2), a court may not impose any civil penalty on a person for a violation of section 623(a)(1), unless the person has been enjoined from committing the violation, or ordered not to commit the violation, in an action or proceeding brought by or on behalf of the Federal Trade Commission, and has violated the injunction or order, and the court may not impose any civil penalty for any violation occurring before the date of the violation of the injunction or order.

(b) ENFORCEMENT BY OTHER AGENCIES.—

(1) IN GENERAL.—Subject to subtitle B of the Consumer Financial Protection Act of 2010, compliance with the require-

ments imposed under this title with respect to consumer reporting agencies, persons who use consumer reports from such agencies, persons who furnish information to such agencies, and users of information that are subject to section 615(d) shall be enforced under—

(A) section 8 of the Federal Deposit Insurance Act (12 U.S.C. 1818), by the appropriate Federal banking agency, as defined in section 3(q) of the Federal Deposit Insurance Act (12 U.S.C. 1813(q)), with respect to—

(i) any national bank or State savings association, and any Federal branch or Federal agency of a foreign bank;

(ii) any member bank of the Federal Reserve System (other than a national bank), a branch or agency of a foreign bank (other than a Federal branch, Federal agency, or insured State branch of a foreign bank), a commercial lending company owned or controlled by a foreign bank, and any organization operating under section 25 or 25A of the Federal Reserve Act; and

(iii) any bank or Federal savings association insured by the Federal Deposit Insurance Corporation (other than a member of the Federal Reserve System) and any insured State branch of a foreign bank;

(B) the Federal Credit Union Act (12 U.S.C. 1751 et seq.), by the Administrator of the National Credit Union Administration with respect to any Federal credit union;

(C) subtitle IV of title 49, United States Code, by the Secretary of Transportation, with respect to all carriers subject to the jurisdiction of the Surface Transportation Board;

(D) the Federal Aviation Act of 1958 (49 U.S.C. App. 1301 et seq.), by the Secretary of Transportation, with respect to any air carrier or foreign air carrier subject to that Act;

(E) the Packers and Stockyards Act, 1921 (7 U.S.C. 181 et seq.) (except as provided in section 406 of that Act), by the Secretary of Agriculture, with respect to any activities subject to that Act;

(F) the Commodity Exchange Act, with respect to a person subject to the jurisdiction of the Commodity Futures Trading Commission;

(G) the Federal securities laws, and any other laws that are subject to the jurisdiction of the Securities and Exchange Commission, with respect to a person that is subject to the jurisdiction of the Securities and Exchange Commission; and

(H) subtitle E of the Consumer Financial Protection Act of 2010, by the Bureau, with respect to any person subject to this title.

(2) INCORPORATED DEFINITIONS.—The terms used in paragraph (1) that are not defined in this title or otherwise defined in section 3(s) of the Federal Deposit Insurance Act (12 U.S.C.

1813(s)) have the same meanings as in section 1(b) of the International Banking Act of 1978 (12 U.S.C. 3101).

(c) STATE ACTION FOR VIOLATIONS.—

(1) AUTHORITY OF STATES.—In addition to such other remedies as are provided under State law, if the chief law enforcement officer of a State, or an official or agency designated by a State, has reason to believe that any person has violated or is violating this title, the State—

(A) may bring an action to enjoin such violation in any appropriate United States district court or in any other court of competent jurisdiction;

(B) subject to paragraph (5), may bring an action on behalf of the residents of the State to recover—

(i) damages for which the person is liable to such residents under sections 616 and 617 as a result of the violation;

(ii) in the case of a violation described in any of paragraphs (1) through (3) of section 623(c), damages for which the person would, but for section 623(c), be liable to such residents as a result of the violation; or

(iii) damages of not more than $1,000 for each willful or negligent violation; and

(C) in the case of any successful action under subparagraph (A) or (B), shall be awarded the costs of the action and reasonable attorney fees as determined by the court.

(2) RIGHTS OF FEDERAL REGULATORS.—The State shall serve prior written notice of any action under paragraph (1) upon the Bureau and the Federal Trade Commission or the appropriate Federal regulator determined under subsection (b) and provide the Bureau and the Federal Trade Commission or appropriate Federal regulator with a copy of its complaint, except in any case in which such prior notice is not feasible, in which case the State shall serve such notice immediately upon instituting such action. The Bureau and the Federal Trade Commission or appropriate Federal regulator shall have the right—

(A) to intervene in the action;

(B) upon so intervening, to be heard on all matters arising therein;

(C) to remove the action to the appropriate United States district court; and

(D) to file petitions for appeal.

(3) INVESTIGATORY POWERS.—For purposes of bringing any action under this subsection, nothing in this subsection shall prevent the chief law enforcement officer, or an official or agency designated by a State, from exercising the powers conferred on the chief law enforcement officer or such official by the laws of such State to conduct investigations or to administer oaths or affirmations or to compel the attendance of witnesses or the production of documentary and other evidence.

(4) LIMITATION ON STATE ACTION WHILE FEDERAL ACTION PENDING.—If the Bureau, the Federal Trade Commission, or the appropriate Federal regulator has instituted a civil action or an administrative action under section 8 of the Federal De-

posit Insurance Act for a violation of this title, no State may, during the pendency of such action, bring an action under this section against any defendant named in the complaint of the Bureau, the Federal Trade Commission, or the appropriate Federal regulator for any violation of this title that is alleged in that complaint.

(5) LIMITATIONS ON STATE ACTIONS FOR CERTAIN VIOLATIONS.—

(A) VIOLATION OF INJUNCTION REQUIRED.—A State may not bring an action against a person under paragraph (1)(B) for a violation described in any of paragraphs (1) through (3) of section 623(c), unless—

(i) the person has been enjoined from committing the violation, in an action brought by the State under paragraph (1)(A); and

(ii) the person has violated the injunction.

(B) LIMITATION ON DAMAGES RECOVERABLE.—In an action against a person under paragraph (1)(B) for a violation described in any of paragraphs (1) through (3) of section 623(c), a State may not recover any damages incurred before the date of the violation of an injunction on which the action is based.

(d) For the purpose of the exercise by any agency referred to in subsection (b) of its powers under any Act referred to in that subsection, a violation of any requirement imposed under this title shall be deemed to be a violation of a requirement imposed under that Act. In addition to its powers under any provision of law specifically referred to in subsection (b), each of the agencies referred to in that subsection may exercise, for the purpose of enforcing compliance with any requirement imposed under this title any other authority conferred on it by law.

(e) REGULATORY AUTHORITY.—

(1) IN GENERAL.—The Bureau shall prescribe such regulations as are necessary to carry out the purposes of this title, except with respect to sections 615(e) and 628. The Bureau may prescribe regulations as may be necessary or appropriate to administer and carry out the purposes and objectives of this title, and to prevent evasions thereof or to facilitate compliance therewith. Except as provided in section 1029(a) of the Consumer Financial Protection Act of 2010, the regulations prescribed by the Bureau under this title shall apply to any person that is subject to this title, notwithstanding the enforcement authorities granted to other agencies under this section.

(2) DEFERENCE.—Notwithstanding any power granted to any Federal agency under this title, the deference that a court affords to a Federal agency with respect to a determination made by such agency relating to the meaning or interpretation of any provision of this title that is subject to the jurisdiction of such agency shall be applied as if that agency were the only agency authorized to apply, enforce, interpret, or administer the provisions of this title The regulations prescribed by the Bureau under this title shall apply to any person that is subject to this title, notwithstanding the enforcement authorities granted to other agencies under this section.

(f) COORDINATION OF CONSUMER COMPLAINT INVESTIGATIONS.—
(1) IN GENERAL.—Each consumer reporting agency described in section 603(p) shall develop and maintain procedures for the referral to each other such agency of any consumer complaint received by the agency alleging identity theft, or requesting a fraud alert under section 605A or a block under section 605B.

(2) MODEL FORM AND PROCEDURE FOR REPORTING IDENTITY THEFT.—The Commission, in consultation with the Federal Trade Commission, the Federal banking agencies, and the National Credit Union Administration, shall develop a model form and model procedures to be used by consumers who are victims of identity theft for contacting and informing creditors and consumer reporting agencies of the fraud.

(3) ANNUAL SUMMARY REPORTS.—Each consumer reporting agency described in section 603(p) shall submit an annual summary report to the Bureau on consumer complaints received by the agency on identity theft or fraud alerts.

(g) BUREAU REGULATION OF CODING OF TRADE NAMES.—If the Bureau determines that a person described in paragraph (9) of section 623(a) has not met the requirements of such paragraph, the Bureau shall take action to ensure the person's compliance with such paragraph, which may include issuing model guidance or prescribing reasonable policies and procedures, as necessary to ensure that such person complies with such paragraph.

§ 622. [15 U.S.C. 1681s-1] Information on overdue child support obligations

Notwithstanding any other provision of this title, a consumer reporting agency shall include in any consumer report furnished by the agency in accordance with section 604, any information on the failure of the consumer to pay overdue support which—
(1) is provided—
(A) to the consumer reporting agency by a State or local child support enforcement agency; or
(B) to the consumer reporting agency and verified by any local, State, or Federal Government agency; and
(2) antedates the report by 7 years or less.

SEC. 623. [15 U.S.C. 1681s-2] RESPONSIBILITIES OF FURNISHERS OF INFORMATION TO CONSUMER REPORTING AGENCIES.

(a) DUTY OF FURNISHERS OF INFORMATION TO PROVIDE ACCURATE INFORMATION.—
(1) PROHIBITION.—
(A) REPORTING INFORMATION WITH ACTUAL KNOWLEDGE OF ERRORS.—A person shall not furnish any information relating to a consumer to any consumer reporting agency if the person knows or has reasonable cause to believe that the information is inaccurate.
(B) REPORTING INFORMATION AFTER NOTICE AND CONFIRMATION OF ERRORS.—A person shall not furnish information relating to a consumer to any consumer reporting agency if—

(i) the person has been notified by the consumer, at the address specified by the person for such notices, that specific information is inaccurate; and

(ii) the information is, in fact, inaccurate.

(C) NO ADDRESS REQUIREMENT.—A person who clearly and conspicuously specifies to the consumer an address for notices referred to in subparagraph (B) shall not be subject to subparagraph (A); however, nothing in subparagraph (B) shall require a person to specify such an address.

(D) DEFINITION.—For purposes of subparagraph (A), the term "reasonable cause to believe that the information is inaccurate" means having specific knowledge, other than solely allegations by the consumer, that would cause a reasonable person to have substantial doubts about the accuracy of the information.

(E) REHABILITATION OF PRIVATE EDUCATION LOANS.—

(i) IN GENERAL.—Notwithstanding any other provision of this section, a consumer may request a financial institution to remove from a consumer report a reported default regarding a private education loan, and such information shall not be considered inaccurate, if—

(I) the financial institution chooses to offer a loan rehabilitation program which includes, without limitation, a requirement of the consumer to make consecutive on-time monthly payments in a number that demonstrates, in the assessment of the financial institution offering the loan rehabilitation program, a renewed ability and willingness to repay the loan; and

(II) the requirements of the loan rehabilitation program described in subclause (I) are successfully met.

(ii) BANKING AGENCIES.—

(I) IN GENERAL.—If a financial institution is supervised by a Federal banking agency, the financial institution shall seek written approval concerning the terms and conditions of the loan rehabilitation program described in clause (i) from the appropriate Federal banking agency.

(II) FEEDBACK.—An appropriate Federal banking agency shall provide feedback to a financial institution within 120 days of a request for approval under subclause (I).

(iii) LIMITATION.—

(I) IN GENERAL.—A consumer may obtain the benefits available under this subsection with respect to rehabilitating a loan only 1 time per loan.

(II) RULE OF CONSTRUCTION.—Nothing in this subparagraph may be construed to require a financial institution to offer a loan rehabilitation program or to remove any reported default from a consumer report as a consideration of a loan rehabilitation program, except as described in clause (i).

(iv) DEFINITIONS.—For purposes of this subparagraph—

(I) the term "appropriate Federal banking agency" has the meaning given the term in section 3 of the Federal Deposit Insurance Act (12 U.S.C. 1813); and

(II) the term "private education loan" has the meaning given the term in section 140(a) of the Truth in Lending Act (15 U.S.C. 1650(a)).

(2) DUTY TO CORRECT AND UPDATE INFORMATION.—A person who—

(A) regularly and in the ordinary course of business furnishes information to one or more consumer reporting agencies about the person's transactions or experiences with any consumer; and

(B) has furnished to a consumer reporting agency information that the person determines is not complete or accurate,

shall promptly notify the consumer reporting agency of that determination and provide to the agency any corrections to that information, or any additional information, that is necessary to make the information provided by the person to the agency complete and accurate, and shall not thereafter furnish to the agency any of the information that remains not complete or accurate.

(3) DUTY TO PROVIDE NOTICE OF DISPUTE.—If the completeness or accuracy of any information furnished by any person to any consumer reporting agency is disputed to such person by a consumer, the person may not furnish the information to any consumer reporting agency without notice that such information is disputed by the consumer.

(4) DUTY TO PROVIDE NOTICE OF CLOSED ACCOUNTS.—A person who regularly and in the ordinary course of business furnishes information to a consumer reporting agency regarding a consumer who has a credit account with that person shall notify the agency of the voluntary closure of the account by the consumer, in information regularly furnished for the period in which the account is closed.

(5) DUTY TO PROVIDE NOTICE OF DELINQUENCY OF ACCOUNTS.—(A) IN GENERAL.—A person who furnishes information to a consumer reporting agency regarding a delinquent account being placed for collection, charged to profit or loss, or subjected to any similar action shall, not later than 90 days after furnishing the information, notify the agency of the date of delinquency on the account, which shall be the month and year of the commencement of the delinquency on the account that immediately preceded the action.

(B) RULE OF CONSTRUCTION.—For purposes of this paragraph only, and provided that the consumer does not dispute the information, a person that furnishes information on a delinquent account that is placed for collection, charged for profit or loss, or subjected to any similar action, complies with this paragraph, if—

(i) the person reports the same date of delinquency as that provided by the creditor to which the account was owed at the time at which the commencement of the delinquency occurred, if the creditor previously reported that date of delinquency to a consumer reporting agency;

(ii) the creditor did not previously report the date of delinquency to a consumer reporting agency, and the person establishes and follows reasonable procedures to obtain the date of delinquency from the creditor or another reliable source and reports that date to a consumer reporting agency as the date of delinquency; or

(iii) the creditor did not previously report the date of delinquency to a consumer reporting agency and the date of delinquency cannot be reasonably obtained as provided in clause (ii), the person establishes and follows reasonable procedures to ensure the date reported as the date of delinquency precedes the date on which the account is placed for collection, charged to profit or loss, or subjected to any similar action, and reports such date to the credit reporting agency.

(6) DUTIES OF FURNISHERS UPON NOTICE OF IDENTITY THEFT-RELATED INFORMATION.—

(A) REASONABLE PROCEDURES.—A person that furnishes information to any consumer reporting agency shall have in place reasonable procedures to respond to any notification that it receives from a consumer reporting agency under section 605B relating to information resulting from identity theft, to prevent that person from refurnishing such blocked information.

(B) INFORMATION ALLEGED TO RESULT FROM IDENTITY THEFT.—If a consumer submits an identity theft report to a person who furnishes information to a consumer reporting agency at the address specified by that person for receiving such reports stating that information maintained by such person that purports to relate to the consumer resulted from identity theft, the person may not furnish such information that purports to relate to the consumer to any consumer reporting agency, unless the person subsequently knows or is informed by the consumer that the information is correct.

(7) NEGATIVE INFORMATION.—

(A) NOTICE TO CONSUMER REQUIRED.—

(i) IN GENERAL.—If any financial institution that extends credit and regularly and in the ordinary course of business furnishes information to a consumer reporting agency described in section 603(p) furnishes negative information to such an agency regarding credit extended to a customer, the financial institution shall provide a notice of such furnishing of negative information, in writing, to the customer.

(ii) NOTICE EFFECTIVE FOR SUBSEQUENT SUBMISSIONS.—After providing such notice, the financial institution may submit additional negative information to a consumer reporting agency described in section 603(p) with respect to the same transaction, extension of credit, account, or customer without providing additional notice to the customer.

(B) TIME OF NOTICE.—

(i) IN GENERAL.—The notice required under subparagraph (A) shall be provided to the customer prior to, or no later than 30 days after, furnishing the negative information to a consumer reporting agency described in section 603(p).

(ii) COORDINATION WITH NEW ACCOUNT DISCLOSURES.—If the notice is provided to the customer prior to furnishing the negative information to a consumer reporting agency, the notice may not be included in the initial disclosures provided under section 127(a) of the Truth in Lending Act.

(C) COORDINATION WITH OTHER DISCLOSURES.—The notice required under subparagraph (A)—

(i) may be included on or with any notice of default, any billing statement, or any other materials provided to the customer; and

(ii) must be clear and conspicuous.

(D) MODEL DISCLOSURE.—

(i) DUTY OF BUREAU.—The Bureau shall prescribe a brief model disclosure that a financial institution may use to comply with subparagraph (A), which shall not exceed 30 words.

(ii) USE OF MODEL NOT REQUIRED.—No provision of this paragraph may be construed to require a financial institution to use any such model form prescribed by the Bureau.

(iii) COMPLIANCE USING MODEL.—A financial institution shall be deemed to be in compliance with subparagraph (A) if the financial institution uses any model form prescribed by the Bureau under this subparagraph, or the financial institution uses any such model form and rearranges its format.

(E) USE OF NOTICE WITHOUT SUBMITTING NEGATIVE INFORMATION.—No provision of this paragraph shall be construed as requiring a financial institution that has provided a customer with a notice described in subparagraph (A) to furnish negative information about the customer to a consumer reporting agency.

(F) SAFE HARBOR.—A financial institution shall not be liable for failure to perform the duties required by this paragraph if, at the time of the failure, the financial institution maintained reasonable policies and procedures to comply with this paragraph or the financial institution reasonably believed that the institution is prohibited, by law, from contacting the consumer.

(G) DEFINITIONS.—For purposes of this paragraph, the following definitions shall apply:

(i) NEGATIVE INFORMATION.—The term "negative information" means information concerning a customer's delinquencies, late payments, insolvency, or any form of default.

(ii) CUSTOMER; FINANCIAL INSTITUTION.—The terms "customer"[5] and "financial institution" have the same meanings as in section 509[6] Public Law 106–102.

(8) ABILITY OF CONSUMER TO DISPUTE INFORMATION DIRECTLY WITH FURNISHER.—

(A) IN GENERAL.—The Bureau shall, in consultation with the Federal Trade Commission, the Federal banking agencies, and the National Credit Union Administration, prescribe regulations that shall identify the circumstances under which a furnisher shall be required to reinvestigate a dispute concerning the accuracy of information contained in a consumer report on the consumer, based on a direct request of a consumer.

(B) CONSIDERATIONS.—In prescribing regulations under subparagraph (A), the agencies shall weigh—

(i) the benefits to consumers with the costs on furnishers and the credit reporting system;

(ii) the impact on the overall accuracy and integrity of consumer reports of any such requirements;

(iii) whether direct contact by the consumer with the furnisher would likely result in the most expeditious resolution of any such dispute; and

(iv) the potential impact on the credit reporting process if credit repair organizations, as defined in section 403(3), including entities that would be a credit repair organization, but for section 403(3)(B)(i), are able to circumvent the prohibition in subparagraph (G).

(C) APPLICABILITY.—Subparagraphs (D) through (G) shall apply in any circumstance identified under the regulations promulgated under subparagraph (A).

(D) SUBMITTING A NOTICE OF DISPUTE.—A consumer who seeks to dispute the accuracy of information shall provide a dispute notice directly to such person at the address specified by the person for such notices that—

(i) identifies the specific information that is being disputed;

(ii) explains the basis for the dispute; and

(iii) includes all supporting documentation required by the furnisher to substantiate the basis of the dispute.

---

[5] Section 509 of Public Law 106–102 does not define "customer" but instead defines "consumer". It is likely the intent was to cross-reference the term "consumer", but note that the term "consumer" is already defined for purposes of this Act (see section 603(c) of this Act), and that definition is different than the definition provided under section 509 of such Public Law.

[6] The lack of the word "of" after "section 509" is so in law.

(E) DUTY OF PERSON AFTER RECEIVING NOTICE OF DISPUTE.—After receiving a notice of dispute from a consumer pursuant to subparagraph (D), the person that provided the information in dispute to a consumer reporting agency shall—

(i) conduct an investigation with respect to the disputed information;

(ii) review all relevant information provided by the consumer with the notice;

(iii) complete such person's investigation of the dispute and report the results of the investigation to the consumer before the expiration of the period under section 611(a)(1) within which a consumer reporting agency would be required to complete its action if the consumer had elected to dispute the information under that section; and

(iv) if the investigation finds that the information reported was inaccurate, promptly notify each consumer reporting agency to which the person furnished the inaccurate information of that determination and provide to the agency any correction to that information that is necessary to make the information provided by the person accurate.

(F) FRIVOLOUS OR IRRELEVANT DISPUTE.—

(i) IN GENERAL.—This paragraph shall not apply if the person receiving a notice of a dispute from a consumer reasonably determines that the dispute is frivolous or irrelevant, including—

(I) by reason of the failure of a consumer to provide sufficient information to investigate the disputed information; or

(II) the submission by a consumer of a dispute that is substantially the same as a dispute previously submitted by or for the consumer, either directly to the person or through a consumer reporting agency under subsection (b), with respect to which the person has already performed the person's duties under this paragraph or subsection (b), as applicable.

(ii) NOTICE OF DETERMINATION.—Upon making any determination under clause (i) that a dispute is frivolous or irrelevant, the person shall notify the consumer of such determination not later than 5 business days after making such determination, by mail or, if authorized by the consumer for that purpose, by any other means available to the person.

(iii) CONTENTS OF NOTICE.—A notice under clause (ii) shall include—

(I) the reasons for the determination under clause (i); and

(II) identification of any information required to investigate the disputed information, which may consist of a standardized form describing the general nature of such information.

(G) EXCLUSION OF CREDIT REPAIR ORGANIZATIONS.—This paragraph shall not apply if the notice of the dispute is submitted by, is prepared on behalf of the consumer by, or is submitted on a form supplied to the consumer by, a credit repair organization, as defined in section 403(3), or an entity that would be a credit repair organization, but for section 403(3)(B)(i).

(9) DUTY TO PROVIDE NOTICE OF STATUS AS MEDICAL INFORMATION FURNISHER.—A person whose primary business is providing medical services, products, or devices, or the person's agent or assignee, who furnishes information to a consumer reporting agency on a consumer shall be considered a medical information furnisher for purposes of this title, and shall notify the agency of such status.

(b) DUTIES OF FURNISHERS OF INFORMATION UPON NOTICE OF DISPUTE.—

(1) IN GENERAL.—After receiving notice pursuant to section 611(a)(2) of a dispute with regard to the completeness or accuracy of any information provided by a person to a consumer reporting agency, the person shall—

(A) conduct an investigation with respect to the disputed information;

(B) review all relevant information provided by the consumer reporting agency pursuant to section 611(a)(2);

(C) report the results of the investigation to the consumer reporting agency;

(D) if the investigation finds that the information is incomplete or inaccurate, report those results to all other consumer reporting agencies to which the person furnished the information and that compile and maintain files on consumers on a nationwide basis; and

(E) if an item of information disputed by a consumer is found to be inaccurate or incomplete or cannot be verified after any reinvestigation under paragraph (1), for purposes of reporting to a consumer reporting agency only, as appropriate, based on the results of the reinvestigation promptly—

(i) modify that item of information;

(ii) delete that item of information; or

(iii) permanently block the reporting of that item of information.

(2) DEADLINE.—A person shall complete all investigations, reviews, and reports required under paragraph (1) regarding information provided by the person to a consumer reporting agency, before the expiration of the period under section 611(a)(1) within which the consumer reporting agency is required to complete actions required by that section regarding that information.

(c) LIMITATION ON LIABILITY.—Except as provided in section 621(c)(1)(B), sections 616 and 617 do not apply to any violation of—

(1) subsection (a) of this section, including any regulations issued thereunder;

(2) subsection (e) of this section, except that nothing in this paragraph shall limit, expand, or otherwise affect liability

under section 616 or 617, as applicable, for violations of subsection (b) of this section; or

(3) subsection (e) of section 615.

(d) LIMITATION ON ENFORCEMENT.—The provisions of law described in paragraphs (1) through (3) of subsection (c) (other than with respect to the exception described in paragraph (2) of subsection (c)) shall be enforced exclusively as provided under section 621 by the Federal agencies and officials and the State officials identified in section 621.

(e) ACCURACY GUIDELINES AND REGULATIONS REQUIRED.—

(1) GUIDELINES.—The Bureau shall, with respect to persons or entities that are subject to the enforcement authority of the Bureau under section 621—

(A) establish and maintain guidelines for use by each person that furnishes information to a consumer reporting agency regarding the accuracy and integrity of the information relating to consumers that such entities furnish to consumer reporting agencies, and update such guidelines as often as necessary; and

(B) prescribe regulations requiring each person that furnishes information to a consumer reporting agency to establish reasonable policies and procedures for implementing the guidelines established pursuant to subparagraph (A).

(2) CRITERIA.—In developing the guidelines required by paragraph (1)(A), the Bureau shall—

(A) identify patterns, practices, and specific forms of activity that can compromise the accuracy and integrity of information furnished to consumer reporting agencies;

(B) review the methods (including technological means) used to furnish information relating to consumers to consumer reporting agencies;

(C) determine whether persons that furnish information to consumer reporting agencies maintain and enforce policies to ensure the accuracy and integrity of information furnished to consumer reporting agencies; and

(D) examine the policies and processes that persons that furnish information to consumer reporting agencies employ to conduct reinvestigations and correct inaccurate information relating to consumers that has been furnished to consumer reporting agencies.

§ 624. Affiliate sharing

(a) SPECIAL RULE FOR SOLICITATION FOR PURPOSES OF MARKETING.—

(1) NOTICE.—Any person that receives from another person related to it by common ownership or affiliated by corporate control a communication of information that would be a consumer report, but for clauses (i), (ii), and (iii) of section 603(d)(2)(A), may not use the information to make a solicitation for marketing purposes to a consumer about its products or services, unless—

(A) it is clearly and conspicuously disclosed to the consumer that the information may be communicated among such persons for purposes of making such solicitations to the consumer; and

(B) the consumer is provided an opportunity and a simple method to prohibit the making of such solicitations to the consumer by such person.

(2) CONSUMER CHOICE.—

(A) IN GENERAL.—The notice required under paragraph (1) shall allow the consumer the opportunity to prohibit all solicitations referred to in such paragraph, and may allow the consumer to choose from different options when electing to prohibit the sending of such solicitations, including options regarding the types of entities and information covered, and which methods of delivering solicitations the consumer elects to prohibit.

(B) FORMAT.—Notwithstanding subparagraph (A), the notice required under paragraph (1) shall be clear, conspicuous, and concise, and any method provided under paragraph (1)(B) shall be simple. The regulations prescribed to implement this section shall provide specific guidance regarding how to comply with such standards.

(3) DURATION.—

(A) IN GENERAL.—The election of a consumer pursuant to paragraph (1)(B) to prohibit the making of solicitations shall be effective for at least 5 years, beginning on the date on which the person receives the election of the consumer, unless the consumer requests that such election be revoked.

(B) NOTICE UPON EXPIRATION OF EFFECTIVE PERIOD.—At such time as the election of a consumer pursuant to paragraph (1)(B) is no longer effective, a person may not use information that the person receives in the manner described in paragraph (1) to make any solicitation for marketing purposes to the consumer, unless the consumer receives a notice and an opportunity, using a simple method, to extend the opt-out for another period of at least 5 years, pursuant to the procedures described in paragraph (1).

(4) SCOPE.—This section shall not apply to a person—

(A) using information to make a solicitation for marketing purposes to a consumer with whom the person has a pre-existing business relationship;

(B) using information to facilitate communications to an individual for whose benefit the person provides employee benefit or other services pursuant to a contract with an employer related to and arising out of the current employment relationship or status of the individual as a participant or beneficiary of an employee benefit plan;

(C) using information to perform services on behalf of another person related by common ownership or affiliated by corporate control, except that this subparagraph shall not be construed as permitting a person to send solicitations on behalf of another person, if such other person would not be permitted to send the solicitation on its own behalf as a result of the election of the consumer to prohibit solicitations under paragraph (1)(B);

(D) using information in response to a communication initiated by the consumer;

(E) using information in response to solicitations authorized or requested by the consumer; or

(F) if compliance with this section by that person would prevent compliance by that person with any provision of State insurance laws pertaining to unfair discrimination in any State in which the person is lawfully doing business.

(5) NO RETROACTIVITY.—This subsection shall not prohibit the use of information to send a solicitation to a consumer if such information was received prior to the date on which persons are required to comply with regulations implementing this subsection.

(b) NOTICE FOR OTHER PURPOSES PERMISSIBLE.—A notice or other disclosure under this section may be coordinated and consolidated with any other notice required to be issued under any other provision of law by a person that is subject to this section, and a notice or other disclosure that is equivalent to the notice required by subsection (a), and that is provided by a person described in subsection (a) to a consumer together with disclosures required by any other provision of law, shall satisfy the requirements of subsection (a).

(c) USER REQUIREMENTS.—Requirements with respect to the use by a person of information received from another person related to it by common ownership or affiliated by corporate control, such as the requirements of this section, constitute requirements with respect to the exchange of information among persons affiliated by common ownership or common corporate control, within the meaning of section 625(b)(2).

(d) DEFINITIONS.—For purposes of this section, the following definitions shall apply:

(1) PRE-EXISTING BUSINESS RELATIONSHIP.—The term "pre-existing business relationship" means a relationship between a person, or a person's licensed agent, and a consumer, based on—

(A) a financial contract between a person and a consumer which is in force;

(B) the purchase, rental, or lease by the consumer of that person's goods or services, or a financial transaction (including holding an active account or a policy in force or having another continuing relationship) between the consumer and that person during the 18-month period immediately preceding the date on which the consumer is sent a solicitation covered by this section;

(C) an inquiry or application by the consumer regarding a product or service offered by that person, during the 3-month period immediately preceding the date on which the consumer is sent a solicitation covered by this section; or

(D) any other pre-existing customer relationship defined in the regulations implementing this section.

(2) SOLICITATION.—The term "solicitation" means the marketing of a product or service initiated by a person to a par-

ticular consumer that is based on an exchange of information described in subsection (a), and is intended to encourage the consumer to purchase such product or service, but does not include communications that are directed at the general public or determined not to be a solicitation by the regulations prescribed under this section.

§ 625. [15 U.S.C. 1681t] Relation to State laws

(a) IN GENERAL.—Except as provided in subsections (b) and (c), this title does not annul, alter, affect, or exempt any person subject to the provisions of this title from complying with the laws of any State with respect to the collection, distribution, or use of any information on consumers, or for the prevention or mitigation of identity theft, except to the extent that those laws are inconsistent with any provision of this title, and then only to the extent of the inconsistency.

(b) GENERAL EXCEPTIONS.—No requirement or prohibition may be imposed under the laws of any State—

    (1) with respect to any subject matter regulated under—

        (A) subsection (c) or (e) of section 604, relating to the prescreening of consumer reports;

        (B) section 611, relating to the time by which a consumer reporting agency must take any action, including the provision of notification to a consumer or other person, in any procedure related to the disputed accuracy of information in a consumer's file, except that this subparagraph shall not apply to any State law in effect on the date of enactment of the Consumer Credit Reporting Reform Act of 1996;

        (C) subsections (a) and (b) of section 615, relating to the duties of a person who takes any adverse action with respect to a consumer;

        (D) section 615(d), relating to the duties of persons who use a consumer report of a consumer in connection with any credit or insurance transaction that is not initiated by the consumer and that consists of a firm offer of credit or insurance;

        (E) section 605, relating to information contained in consumer reports, except that this subparagraph shall not apply to any State law in effect on the date of enactment of the Consumer Credit Reporting Reform Act of 1996;

        (F) section 623, relating to the responsibilities of persons who furnish information to consumer reporting agencies, except that this paragraph shall not apply—

            (i) with respect to section 54A(a) of chapter 93 of the Massachusetts Annotated Laws (as in effect on the date of enactment of the Consumer Credit Reporting Reform Act of 1996); or

            (ii) with respect to section 1785.25(a) of the California Civil Code (as in effect on the date of enactment of the Consumer Credit Reporting Reform Act of 1996);

        (G) section 609(e), relating to information available to victims under section 609(e);

(H) section 624, relating to the exchange and use of information to make a solicitation for marketing purposes;

(I) section 615(h), relating to the duties of users of consumer reports to provide notice with respect to terms in certain credit transactions;

(J) subsections (i) and (j) of section 605A relating to security freezes; or

(K) subsection (k) of section 605A, relating to credit monitoring for active duty military consumers, as defined in that subsection;

(2) with respect to the exchange of information among persons affiliated by common ownership or common corporate control, except that this paragraph shall not apply with respect to subsection (a) or (c)(1) of section 2480e of title 9, Vermont Statutes Annotated (as in effect on the date of enactment of the Consumer Credit Reporting Reform Act of 1996);

(3) with respect to the disclosures required to be made under subsection (c), (d), (e), or (g) of section 609, or subsection (f) of section 609 relating to the disclosure of credit scores for credit granting purposes, except that this paragraph—

(A) shall not apply with respect to sections 1785.10, 1785.16, and 1785.20.2 of the California Civil Code (as in effect on the date of enactment of the Fair and Accurate Credit Transactions Act of 2003) and section 1785.15 through section 1785.15.2 of such Code (as in effect on such date);

(B) shall not apply with respect to sections 5–3–106(2) and 212–14.3–104.3 of the Colorado Revised Statutes (as in effect on the date of enactment of the Fair and Accurate Credit Transactions Act of 2003); and

(C) shall not be construed as limiting, annulling, affecting, or superseding any provision of the laws of any State regulating the use in an insurance activity, or regulating disclosures concerning such use, of a credit-based insurance score of a consumer by any person engaged in the business of insurance;

(4) with respect to the frequency of any disclosure under section 612(a), except that this paragraph shall not apply—

(A) with respect to section 12–14.3–105(1)(d) of the Colorado Revised Statutes (as in effect on the date of enactment of the Fair and Accurate Credit Transactions Act of 2003);

(B) with respect to section 10–1–393(29)(C) of the Georgia Code (as in effect on the date of enactment of the Fair and Accurate Credit Transactions Act of 2003);

(C) with respect to section 1316.2 of title 10 of the Maine Revised Statutes (as in effect on the date of enactment of the Fair and Accurate Credit Transactions Act of 2003);

(D) with respect to sections 14–1209(a)(1) and 14–1209(b)(1)(i) of the Commercial Law Article of the Code of Maryland (as in effect on the date of enactment of the Fair and Accurate Credit Transactions Act of 2003);

(E) with respect to section 59(d) and section 59(e) of chapter 93 of the General Laws of Massachusetts (as in effect on the date of enactment of the Fair and Accurate Credit Transactions Act of 2003);

(F) with respect to section 56:11–37.10(a)(1) of the New Jersey Revised Statutes (as in effect on the date of enactment of the Fair and Accurate Credit Transactions Act of 2003); or

(G) with respect to section 2480c(a)(1) of title 9 of the Vermont Statutes Annotated (as in effect on the date of enactment of the Fair and Accurate Credit Transactions Act of 2003); or

(5) with respect to the conduct required by the specific provisions of—

(A) section 605(g);
(B) section 605A;
(C) section 605B;
(D) section 609(a)(1)(A);
(E) section 612(a);
(F) subsections (e), (f), and (g) of section 615;
(G) section 621(f);
(H) section 623(a)(6); or
(I) section 628.

(c) DEFINITION OF FIRM OFFER OF CREDIT OR INSURANCE.—Notwithstanding any definition of the term "firm offer of credit or insurance" (or any equivalent term) under the laws of any State, the definition of that term contained in section 603(l) shall be construed to apply in the enforcement and interpretation of the laws of any State governing consumer reports.

(d) LIMITATIONS.—Subsections (b) and (c) do not affect any settlement, agreement, or consent judgment between any State Attorney General and any consumer reporting agency in effect on the date of enactment of the Consumer Credit Reporting Reform Act of 1996.

§ 626. [15 U.S.C. 1681u] Disclosures to FBI for counterintelligence purposes

(a) IDENTITY OF FINANCIAL INSTITUTIONS.—Notwithstanding section 604 or any other provision of this title, a consumer reporting agency shall furnish to the Federal Bureau of Investigation the names and addresses of all financial institutions (as that term is defined in section 1101 of the Right to Financial Privacy Act of 1978) at which a consumer maintains or has maintained an account, to the extent that information is in the files of the agency, when presented with a written request for that information that includes a term that specifically identifies a consumer or account to be used as the basis for the production of that information, signed by the Director of the Federal Bureau of Investigation, or the Director's designee in a position not lower than Deputy Assistant Director at Bureau headquarters or a Special Agent in Charge of a Bureau field office designated by the Director, which certifies compliance with this section. The Director or the Director's designee may make such a certification only if the Director or the Director's designee has determined in writing, that such information is sought for the conduct of an authorized investigation to protect against international terrorism or clandestine intelligence activities, provided that such an investigation of a United States person is not conducted solely upon the basis of activities protected by the first amendment to the Constitution of the United States.

(b) IDENTIFYING INFORMATION.—Notwithstanding the provisions of section 604 or any other provision of this title, a consumer reporting agency shall furnish identifying information respecting a consumer, limited to name, address, former addresses, places of employment, or former places of employment, to the Federal Bureau of Investigation when presented with a written request that includes a term that specifically identifies a consumer or account to be used as the basis for the production of that information, signed by the Director or the Director's designee in a position not lower than Deputy Assistant Director at Bureau headquarters or a Special Agent in Charge of a Bureau field office designated by the Director, which certifies compliance with this subsection. The Director or the Director's designee may make such a certification only if the Director or the Director's designee has determined in writing that such information is sought for the conduct of an authorized investigation to protect against international terrorism or clandestine intelligence activities, provided that such an investigation of a United States person is not conducted solely upon the basis of activities protected by the first amendment to the Constitution of the United States.

[Note: Subsections (a) and (b) of section 626 of the Fair Credit Reporting Act, as they read prior to the enactment of Public Law 107–56 (enacted October 26, 2001) and appeared in a second section designated as section 624, reads as follows:]

(a) IDENTITY OF FINANCIAL INSTITUTIONS.—Notwithstanding section 604 or any other provision of this title, a consumer reporting agency shall furnish to the Federal Bureau of Investigation the names and addresses of all financial institutions (as that term is defined in section 1101 of the Right to Financial Privacy Act of 1978) at which a consumer maintains or has maintained an account, to the extent that information is in the files of the agency, when presented with a written request for that information, signed by the Director of the Federal Bureau of Investigation, or the Director's designee, which certifies compliance with this section. The Director or the Director's designee may make such a certification only if the Director or the Director's designee has determined in writing that—

(1) such information is necessary for the conduct of an authorized foreign counterintelligence investigation; and

(2) there are specific and articulable facts giving reason to believe that the consumer—

(A) is a foreign power (as defined in section 101 of the Foreign Intelligence Surveillance Act of 1978) or a person who is not a United States person (as defined in such section 101) and is an official of a foreign power; or

(B) is an agent of a foreign power and is engaging or has engaged in an act of international terrorism (as that

term is defined in section 101(c) of the Foreign Intelligence Surveillance Act of 1978) or clandestine intelligence activities that involve or may involve a violation of criminal statutes of the United States.

(b) IDENTIFYING INFORMATION.—Notwithstanding the provisions of section 604 or any other provision of this title, a consumer reporting agency shall furnish identifying information respecting a consumer, limited to name, address, former addresses, places of employment, or former places of employment, to the Federal Bureau of Investigation when presented with a written request, signed by the Director or the Director's designee, which certifies compliance with this subsection. The Director or the Director's designee may make such a certification only if the Director or the Director's designee has determined in writing that—

(1) such information is necessary to the conduct of an authorized counterintelligence investigation; and

(2) there is information giving reason to believe that the consumer has been, or is about to be, in contact with a foreign power or an agent of a foreign power (as defined in section 101 of the Foreign Intelligence Surveillance Act of 1978).

(c) COURT ORDER FOR DISCLOSURE OF CONSUMER REPORTS.—Notwithstanding section 604 or any other provision of this title, if requested in writing by the Director of the Federal Bureau of Investigation, or a designee of the Director in a position not lower than Deputy Assistant Director at Bureau headquarters or a Special Agent in Charge in a Bureau field office designated by the Director, a court may issue an order ex parte, which shall include a term that specifically identifies a consumer or account to be used as the basis for the production of the information, directing a consumer reporting agency to furnish a consumer report to the Federal Bureau of Investigation, upon a showing in camera that the consumer report is sought for the conduct of an authorized investigation to protect against international terrorism or clandestine intelligence activities, provided that such an investigation of a United States person is not conducted solely upon the basis of activities protected by the first amendment to the Constitution of the United States. The terms of an order issued under this subsection shall not disclose that the order is issued for purposes of a counterintelligence investigation.

(d) PROHIBITION OF CERTAIN DISCLOSURE.—

(1) PROHIBITION.—

(A) IN GENERAL.—If a certification is issued under subparagraph (B) and notice of the right to judicial review under subsection (e) is provided, no consumer reporting agency that receives a request under subsection (a) or (b) or an order under subsection (c), or officer, employee, or agent thereof, shall disclose or specify in any consumer report, that the Federal Bureau of Investigation has sought or obtained access to information or records under subsection (a), (b), or (c).

(B) CERTIFICATION.—The requirements of subparagraph (A) shall apply if the Director of the Federal Bureau of Investigation, or a designee of the Director whose rank shall be no lower than Deputy Assistant Director at Bureau headquarters or a Special Agent in Charge of a Bureau field office, certifies that the absence of a prohibition of disclosure under this subsection may result in—

(i) a danger to the national security of the United States;

(ii) interference with a criminal, counterterrorism, or counterintelligence investigation;

(iii) interference with diplomatic relations; or

(iv) danger to the life or physical safety of any person.

(2) EXCEPTION.—

(A) IN GENERAL.—A consumer reporting agency that receives a request under subsection (a) or (b) or an order under subsection (c), or officer, employee, or agent thereof, may disclose information otherwise subject to any applicable nondisclosure requirement to—

(i) those persons to whom disclosure is necessary in order to comply with the request;

(ii) an attorney in order to obtain legal advice or assistance regarding the request; or

(iii) other persons as permitted by the Director of the Federal Bureau of Investigation or the designee of the Director.

(B) APPLICATION.—A person to whom disclosure is made under subparagraph (A) shall be subject to the nondisclosure requirements applicable to a person to whom a request under subsection (a) or (b) or an order under subsection (c) is issued in the same manner as the person to whom the request is issued.

(C) NOTICE.—Any recipient that discloses to a person described in subparagraph (A) information otherwise subject to a nondisclosure requirement shall inform the person of the applicable nondisclosure requirement.

(D) IDENTIFICATION OF DISCLOSURE RECIPIENTS.—At the request of the Director of the Federal Bureau of Investigation or the designee of the Director, any person making or intending to make a disclosure under clause (i) or (iii) of subparagraph (A) shall identify to the Director or such designee the person to whom such disclosure will be made or to whom such disclosure was made prior to the request.

(e) JUDICIAL REVIEW.—

(1) IN GENERAL.—A request under subsection (a) or (b) or an order under subsection (c) or a non-disclosure requirement imposed in connection with such request under subsection (d) shall be subject to judicial review under section 3511 of title 18, United States Code.

(2) NOTICE.—A request under subsection (a) or (b) or an order under subsection (c) shall include notice of the availability of judicial review described in paragraph (1).

(f) PAYMENT OF FEES.—The Federal Bureau of Investigation shall, subject to the availability of appropriations, pay to the consumer reporting agency assembling or providing report or information in accordance with procedures established under this section a fee for reimbursement for such costs as are reasonably necessary and which have been directly incurred in searching, reproducing, or transporting books, papers, records, or other data required or requested to be produced under this section.

(g) LIMIT ON DISSEMINATION.—The Federal Bureau of Investigation may not disseminate information obtained pursuant to this section outside of the Federal Bureau of Investigation, except to other Federal agencies as may be necessary for the approval or conduct of a foreign counterintelligence investigation, or, where the information concerns a person subject to the Uniform Code of Military Justice, to appropriate investigative authorities within the military department concerned as may be necessary for the conduct of a joint foreign counterintelligence investigation.

(h) RULES OF CONSTRUCTION.—Nothing in this section shall be construed to prohibit information from being furnished by the Federal Bureau of Investigation pursuant to a subpoena or court order, in connection with a judicial or administrative proceeding to enforce the provisions of this Act. Nothing in this section shall be construed to authorize or permit the withholding of information from the Congress.

(i) REPORTS TO CONGRESS.—(1) On a semiannual basis, the Attorney General shall fully inform the Permanent Select Committee on Intelligence and the Committee on Banking, Finance and Urban Affairs of the House of Representatives, and the Select Committee on Intelligence and the Committee on Banking, Housing, and Urban Affairs of the Senate concerning all requests made pursuant to subsections (a), (b), and (c).

(2) In the case of the semiannual reports required to be submitted under paragraph (1) to the Permanent Select Committee on Intelligence of the House of Representatives and the Select Committee on Intelligence of the Senate, the submittal dates for such reports shall be as provided in section 507 of the National Security Act of 1947.

(j) DAMAGES.—Any agency or department of the United States obtaining or disclosing any consumer reports, records, or information contained therein in violation of this section is liable to the consumer to whom such consumer reports, records, or information relate in an amount equal to the sum of—

(1) $100, without regard to the volume of consumer reports, records, or information involved;

(2) any actual damages sustained by the consumer as a result of the disclosure;

(3) if the violation is found to have been willful or intentional, such punitive damages as a court may allow; and

(4) in the case of any successful action to enforce liability under this subsection, the costs of the action, together with reasonable attorney fees, as determined by the court.

(k) DISCIPLINARY ACTIONS FOR VIOLATIONS.—If a court determines that any agency or department of the United States has violated any provision of this section and the court finds that the circumstances surrounding the violation raise questions of whether or not an officer or employee of the agency or department acted willfully or intentionally with respect to the violation, the agency or department shall promptly initiate a proceeding to determine whether or not disciplinary action is warranted against the officer or employee who was responsible for the violation.

(l) GOOD-FAITH EXCEPTION.—Notwithstanding any other provision of this title, any consumer reporting agency or agent or employee thereof making disclosure of consumer reports or identifying information pursuant to this subsection in good-faith reliance upon a certification of the Federal Bureau of Investigation pursuant to provisions of this section shall not be liable to any person for such disclosure under this title, the constitution of any State, or any law or regulation of any State or any political subdivision of any State.

(m) LIMITATION OF REMEDIES.—Notwithstanding any other provision of this title, the remedies and sanctions set forth in this section shall be the only judicial remedies and sanctions for violation of this section.

(n) INJUNCTIVE RELIEF.—In addition to any other remedy contained in this section, injunctive relief shall be available to require compliance with the procedures of this section. In the event of any successful action under this subsection, costs together with reasonable attorney fees, as determined by the court, may be recovered.

§ 627. [15 U.S.C. 1681v] Disclosures to governmental agencies for counterterrorism purposes

(a) DISCLOSURE.—Notwithstanding section 604 or any other provision of this title, a consumer reporting agency shall furnish a consumer report of a consumer and all other information in a consumer's file to a government agency authorized to conduct investigations of, or intelligence or counterintelligence activities or analysis related to, international terrorism when presented with a written certification by such government agency that such information is necessary for the agency's conduct or such investigation, activity or analysis and that includes a term that specifically identifies a consumer or account to be used as the basis for the production of such information.

(b) FORM OF CERTIFICATION.—The certification described in subsection (a) shall be signed by a supervisory official designated by the head of a Federal agency or an officer of a Federal agency whose appointment to office is required to be made by the President, by and with the advice and consent of the Senate.

(c) PROHIBITION OF CERTAIN DISCLOSURE.—
  (1) PROHIBITION.—
    (A) IN GENERAL.—If a certification is issued under subparagraph (B) and notice of the right to judicial review under subsection (d) is provided, no consumer reporting agency that receives a request under subsection (a), or officer, employee, or agent thereof, shall disclose or specify in any consumer report, that a government agency described in subsection (a) has sought or obtained access to information or records under subsection (a).
    (B) CERTIFICATION.—The requirements of subparagraph (A) shall apply if the head of the government agency described in subsection (a), or a designee, certifies that the absence of a prohibition of disclosure under this subsection may result in—

(i) a danger to the national security of the United States;

(ii) interference with a criminal, counterterrorism, or counterintelligence investigation;

(iii) interference with diplomatic relations; or

(iv) danger to the life or physical safety of any person.

(2) EXCEPTION.—

(A) IN GENERAL.—A consumer reporting agency that receives a request under subsection (a), or officer, employee, or agent thereof, may disclose information otherwise subject to any applicable nondisclosure requirement to—

(i) those persons to whom disclosure is necessary in order to comply with the request;

(ii) an attorney in order to obtain legal advice or assistance regarding the request; or

(iii) other persons as permitted by the head of the government agency described in subsection (a) or a designee.

(B) APPLICATION.—A person to whom disclosure is made under subparagraph (A) shall be subject to the nondisclosure requirements applicable to a person to whom a request under subsection (a) is issued in the same manner as the person to whom the request is issued.

(C) NOTICE.—Any recipient that discloses to a person described in subparagraph (A) information otherwise subject to a nondisclosure requirement shall inform the person of the applicable nondisclosure requirement.

(D) IDENTIFICATION OF DISCLOSURE RECIPIENTS.—At the request of the head of the government agency described in subsection (a) or a designee, any person making or intending to make a disclosure under clause (i) or (iii) of subparagraph (A) shall identify to the head or such designee the person to whom such disclosure will be made or to whom such disclosure was made prior to the request.

(d) JUDICIAL REVIEW.—

(1) IN GENERAL.—A request under subsection (a) or a nondisclosure requirement imposed in connection with such request under subsection (c) shall be subject to judicial review under section 3511 of title 18, United States Code.

(2) NOTICE.—A request under subsection (a) shall include notice of the availability of judicial review described in paragraph (1).

(e) RULE OF CONSTRUCTION.—Nothing in section 626 shall be construed to limit the authority of the Director of the Federal Bureau of Investigation under this section.

(f) SAFE HARBOR.—Notwithstanding any other provision of this title, any consumer reporting agency or agent or employee thereof making disclosure of consumer reports or other information pursuant to this section in good-faith reliance upon a certification of a government agency [7] pursuant to the provisions of this section shall not be liable to any person for such disclosure under this subchapter, the constitution of any State, or any law or regulation of any State or any political subdivision of any State.

(g) REPORTS TO CONGRESS.—(1) On a semi-annual basis, the Attorney General shall fully inform the Committee on the Judiciary, the Committee on Financial Services, and the Permanent Select Committee on Intelligence of the House of Representatives and the Committee on the Judiciary, the Committee on Banking, Housing, and Urban Affairs, and the Select Committee on Intelligence of the Senate concerning all requests made pursuant to subsection (a).

(2) In the case of the semiannual reports required to be submitted under paragraph (1) to the Permanent Select Committee on Intelligence of the House of Representatives and the Select Committee on Intelligence of the Senate, the submittal dates for such reports shall be as provided in section 507 of the National Security Act of 1947 (50 U.S.C. 415b).

§ 628. [15 U.S.C. 1681w] Disposal of records

(a) REGULATIONS.—

(1) IN GENERAL.—The Federal Trade Commission, the Securities and Exchange Commission, the Commodity Futures Trading Commission, the Federal banking agencies, and the National Credit Union Administration, with respect to the entities that are subject to their respective enforcement authority under section 621, and in coordination as described in paragraph (2), shall issue final regulations requiring any person that maintains or otherwise possesses consumer information, or any compilation of consumer information, derived from consumer reports for a business purpose to properly dispose of any such information or compilation.

(2) COORDINATION.—Each agency required to prescribe regulations under paragraph (1) shall—

(A) consult and coordinate with each other such agency so that, to the extent possible, the regulations prescribed by each such agency are consistent and comparable with the regulations by each such other agency; and

(B) ensure that such regulations are consistent with the requirements and regulations issued pursuant to Public Law 106–102 and other provisions of Federal law.

(3) EXEMPTION AUTHORITY.—In issuing regulations under this section, the agencies identified in paragraph (1) may exempt any person or class of persons from application of those regulations, as such agency deems appropriate to carry out the purpose of this section.

(b) RULE OF CONSTRUCTION.—Nothing in this section shall be construed—

---

[7] The amendment made by section 6203(l) of Public Law 108–458 (118 Stat. 3747) to "[s]ection 626(e) of the Fair Credit Reporting Act (15 U.S.C. 1681v(e))" to strike "governmental agency" and insert "government agency" was executed to section 627(e) (as redesignated by section 214(a)(1) of Public Law 108–159; 117 Stat. 1980) to reflect the probable intent of the Congress.

(1) to require a person to maintain or destroy any record pertaining to a consumer that is not imposed under other law; or

(2) to alter or affect any requirement imposed under any other provision of law to maintain or destroy such a record.

§ 629. [15 U.S.C. 1681x] Corporate and technological circumvention prohibited

The Commission shall prescribe regulations, to become effective not later than 90 days after the date of enactment of this section, to prevent a consumer reporting agency from circumventing or evading treatment as a consumer reporting agency described in section 603(p) for purposes of this title, including—

(1) by means of a corporate reorganization or restructuring, including a merger, acquisition, dissolution, divestiture, or asset sale of a consumer reporting agency; or

(2) by maintaining or merging public record and credit account information in a manner that is substantially equivalent to that described in paragraphs (1) and (2) of section 603(p), in the manner described in section 603(p).

Made in the USA
Coppell, TX
15 January 2021